Heavenly Foods

Hajjah Nazihe Adil Kabbani

Edited & Annotated by Sonia Shaikh

© **Copyright 2006 by the Institute for Spiritual and Cultural Advancement.**
All rights reserved. Published 2006.

ISBN: 1-930409-44-3

No part of this book may be reproduced, stored in a retrieval system, or transmitted in any form, or by any means, electronic, mechanical, photocopying, or otherwise, without the written permission of the Islamic Supreme Council of America.

Published and Distributed by:
Institute for Spiritual and Cultural Advancement
17195 Silver Parkway, #201
Fenton, MI 48430 USA
Tel: (888) 278-6624
Fax: (810) 815-0518

Disclaimer
The following is a rough draft of Hajjah Naziha's upcoming cookbook, *Heavenly Foods*.
Hajjah Naziha wanted to make these recipes available before Ramadan.
Please e-mail any questions or comments to The Editor at staff@naqshbandi.org.
Thank You.

Dedication

My mother, Hajjah Amina Adil, and mother-in-law, Hajjah Yousra Kabbani, have both passed from their earthly existence. They are the two women who taught me how to cook. I ask that every time you cook, you read Surat al-Fatiha for both Hajjah Amina-and Hajjah Yousra. I learned to cook all the Lebanese food from Hajjah Yousra. My mother-in-law was also very considerate, and would cook for everyone in the house whatever they liked to eat. I learned from my mother, the wife of H.E. Mawlana Shaykh Nazim the duties as the wife of a shaykh, including how to cook for a large number of people. My mother-in-law was an excellent entertainer who would host many people. It is my great honor to follow in the footsteps of these two great women.
I would like to also express my sincere thanks to Sonia Shaikh and to all the ladies helping in the *zawiya* kitchen, in particular Hadieh Khan, for their help in preparing this book.

Sincerely,

Hajjah Nazihe Adil Kabbani

Contents

Dedication 3
About Hajjah Naziha 9
Supplications 10
    Du'a Before Eating 10
    Du'a After Eating 11
Soup Chapter 12
    The Soup of Fatima az-Zahra 12
    Lentil Soup 14
    Meatball and Noodle Soup 17
    Tortellini Soup 19
    Brown Lentil and Cumin Soup 22
    Cheese Soup 24
Appetizer Chapter 25
    The Eggplant 25
    Roasted Eggplant Spread 26
    Garbanzo and Tahini Spread 29
    Garbanzo and Tahini Spread with Ground Beef 31
Salad Chapter 32
    Hajjah Naziha: Her Parents' Helper 32
    Everyday Mixed Salad 33
    Crispy Bread and Green Salad in Tangy Garlic Dressing 35
    Tomato and Onion Salad 37
    Yogurt and Cucumber Salad 38

    Russian Salad 39

    Tangy Brown Lentil and Garlic Salad 40

    Tangy White Bean and Onion Salad 41

Bean Chapter 43

    The Blessings of Guests 43

    Cumin Seasoned Old World Lentils 44

    White Beans and Carrots 47

Vegetable Sides Chapter 49

    The Purity of Hajjah Naziha 49

    Leeks and Tomatoes 50

    Fried Okra and Tomatoes 52

    Stuffed Green Peppers with Coriander Seeds and Garlic 54

    Carrots, Brussel Sprouts, and Broccoli 56

    Zucchini with Yogurt Sauce 58

    Eggplant with Yogurt and Garlic 60

    Portuguese Potatoes 62

    Home Style French Fries 63

Rice Chapter 64

    The Stingy Man and the Generous Man 64

    Leeks with Rice and Carrots 65

    Rice Pilaf with Meat Chunks and Carrots 67

    Perfect Rice Pilaf 70

Savory Pastry Chapter 71

    The Salt and Sayyidina Ibrahim 71

    Ground Beef Pastry Squares 72

    Triangle Spinach Pies 76

    Cheese-Filled Pastry Squares 80

    Golden Half-Moon Beef Pastries 85

    Savory Rice with Beef and Nuts Enveloped in Phyllo Pastry 87

Chicken and Fish Chapter 94

    Advice on Eating with Children 94

    Chicken and Potatoes 95

    Fried Chicken 98

    Indonesian Chicken 100

    Rosemary Chicken with Garlic 102

    Salmon with Mashed Potatoes 103

Meat Chapter 105

    Hajjah Amina's *Baraka* 105

    Leg of Lamb 106

    Leg of Lamb with Spring Vegetables 107

    Grandshaykh's Dish: Tender Peppered Beef Smothered in Succulent Onions 109

    Meat Dumplings 111

    Ravioli with Yogurt 114

    Eggplant Stuffed with Lamb 117

    Stuffed Mushrooms with Ground Beef 120

    Stuffed Tomatoes with Green Bell Peppers 122

    Stuffed Zucchini and Eggplant 124

    Meatloaf with Eggs and Peas 126

    Kafta with Potatoes 129

    Savory Ground Beef with Tomato Wedges 131

    Ground Beef and Spaghetti Casserole 132

    Meat and Potato Pie 135

Braise Chapter 138

    Spinach and Meatball Braise 139

    Flat Green Bean and Beef Chunk Braise 141

    Green Beans and Meat Chunk Braise 143

    Molokhiya with Beef Chunk Braise 144

    Eggplant with Meat Chunk Braise 147

Dessert Chapter 149

    Hajjah Naziha's Young Mind 149

    Rice Pudding 150

    Baked Apples and Pears 152

    Stuffed Oranges with Orange Sorbet 154

    Coconut Pudding 156

    Apricot Compote 158

    Milk and Orange Layered Upside-Down Pudding 160

    Chocolate Dream Cake 162

    Swiss Roll 164

    Burnt Milk Pudding with Chicken Breasts 165

Beverage Chapter 167

    Zam Zam Water 167

    Arabic Coffee 168

كُلُوا وَاشْرَبُوا هَنِيئًا بِمَا كُنتُمْ تَعْمَلُونَ

(To them will be said:) "Eat and drink ye, with profit and health, because of your (good) deeds."
Holy Qur'an Surat at-Tur, 52:19

About Hajjah Naziha

Hajjah Naziha Adil was born into a unique household, which existed and exists for and in the service of Allah. As a young child, she lived next door to Grandshaykh Abdullah Daghestani ق of the Naqshbandi tariqah. Upon his passing, her father, Mawlana Shaykh Nazim became the grandshaykh of the tariqah. Her mother is Hajjah Amina Adil ق, a scholar of Islam, who taught and wrote extensively on the lives of the Prophets.

Hajjah Naziha's life has not been an easy one, but it has been filled with the honor and dignity of service in many forms. From the time she was ten, travelers who came to Grandshaykh Abdullah ق would throw their dirty clothes over a fence and she and her mother, Hajjah Amina ق, would scrub them. She also helped her mother cook for the Shaykh and the students streaming in and out of his house every day.

They worked very hard in the household of their Shaykh - not receiving money or accolades but to serve Allah Ta'ala. When she had free time, she would run to the house of Grandshaykh Abdullah ق and listen to his lectures. Before his passing, Grandshaykh Abdullah ق married her to Shaykh Hisham Kabbani.

She is a descendant of the Prophet Muhammad ﷺ on both her paternal and maternal sides. She has traveled the world – Europe, the Middle East, the Far East and Alaska – with her parents and husband, doing *dhikr* and bringing people back in touch with their spiritual selves, with their origin. She has observed many people, cultures, and personal situations, and advises women around the world on a variety of topics.

Thus, she has been in the households of four scholars, and through her diligence and constant association has become a scholar and advisor herself. Before his passing, Grandshayh Abdullah ق decreed that she would be a teacher for women, and this is what has come to pass. May Allah Ta'ala shower her and her family with blessings evermore, and grant them long life and good health.

Supplications

Du'a Before Eating

أَشْهَدُ أَنْ لا إِلَهَ إِلاَّ الله وَأَشْهَدُ أَنَّ مُحَمَّداً عَبْدُهُ وَرَسُولُهُ – أَسْتَغْفِرُ اللهَ العَظيم 3×

فَإِن تَوَلَّوْا فَقُلْ حَسْبِيَ اللهُ لا إِلَهَ إِلاَّ هُوَ عَلَيْهِ تَوَكَّلْتُ وَهُوَ رَبُّ الْعَرْشِ الْعَظيم

إِلى شَرَفِ النَبِي صَلى الله عَلَيْهِ وَ سَلَم وَآلِه وَأَصْحَابِه الكِرَام، وَإِلى أرْواحِ آبَائِنا وَأَمَّهاتِنا وَ حَضْرَةِ أُسْتاذِنا

وَأُسْتاذِ أُسْتاذِنا والصِدَيقِين الفَاتِحَة

Ash-hadu an lā ilāha illa-Allāh wa ash-hadu anna Muḥammadan ʿabduhu wa-rasūluhu, Astaghfirullāhu 'l-ʿAẓīm (3x)
Fa in tawallaw faqul ḥasbīy-Allāhu lā ilāha illa Hūw. ʿalayhi tawakaltu wa Hūwa rabbu 'l-ʿarshi 'l-ʿaẓīm.
Ila sharafi 'n-Nabī ṣall-Allāhu ʿalayhi wa sallam, wa ālihi wa aṣḥābihi 'l-kirām wa ila arwāḥi ābāʾinā wa ummuhātinā wa ḥaḍrati ustādhinā wa ustādhi ustādhinā wa 'ṣ-ṣiddīqīyyīn al-fātiḥa.

I bear witness that there is no god but Allah and I bear witness that Muhammad is His Slave and Messenger; I ask forgiveness from Allah (3x)
But if they turn away, Say: "(Allah) is sufficient for me: there is no god but He: in Him I place my trust – and He is the Lord of the Throne Supreme."
We send this (as an offering) to the Honored Prophet (s), to his family and his companions; and to the souls of our fathers, our mothers, our venerated teachers and the teachers of our teachers, and the veracious ones. (Recite) *Surat al-Fatiha.*

Du'a After Eating

الحَمْدُ لله الَذي أطعَمَنا وَسَقانا وَجَعَلَنا مُسْلِمين، الحَمْدُ لله حَمْدا يُوافي نِعمَهُ وَيُكافي مَزيدَهُ كَما يَنْبَغي لِجَلالِ وَجهِكَ العَظيم يَا اللهُ، نِعمَة جَليل الله بَرَكَة خَليل الله شَفاعَة يَا رَسُولُ الله، اللّهُمَّ أَكرِم صاحِب هَذا الطَّعام والآكِلين، اللهم زِد وَ لا تُقَلِّل إلى شَرَفِ النَبي صَلى الله عَلَيه وَ سَلَم وآلِه وأصحابِه الكِرام وَ حَضرَة أُستاذَنا وَأُستاذ أُستاذَنا والصديقِين ربنا تقبل منا بحرمة سر سورة الفاتحة.

Alḥamdulillāhi 'lladhī aṭ'amanā wa saqānā wa j'alanā muslimīna. Alḥamdulillāh ḥamdan yuwāfi n'imahu wa yukāfi mazīdahu kamā yanbaghī li-jalāli wajhika 'l-'adhīm yā Allāh, n'ima jalīlullāh, barakat khalīlullāh, shafa'at yā rasūlullāh, Allāhuma 'krim ṣāḥib hadhā-ṭ-ṭ'am wa'l-ākilīn. Allāhuma zid wal ā tuqallil ila sharafi'n-Nabī ṣall-Allāhu 'alayhi wa sallam, wa ālihi wa aṣḥābihi 'l-kirām wa ila arwāḥi ābā'inā wa ummuhātinā wa ḥadrati ustādhinā wa ustādhi ustādhinā wa 'ṣ-ṣiddīqīyyīn. Rabbanā taqabbal minnā bi-ḥurmati sirri sūratu'l-fātiḥa.

Praise be to Allah who fed us, who quenched our thirst, and who made us to be Muslims. Praise be to Allah, a praise such that it equals to His favors, and meets His increase (of His favors); a praise which is adequate to the magnificence of your Magnificent Countenance. (Grant us) the favors of the mighty one of Allah, the blessings of the intimate friend of Allah, the intercession of the Messenger of Allah. Oh Allah honor the owner of this food and those who are eating from it. Oh Allah increase and do not diminish. We send this (as an offering) to the Honored Prophet ﷺ, to his family and his companions; and to the souls of our fathers, our mothers, our venerated teachers and the teachers of our teachers, and the veracious ones. (Recite) *Surat al- Fatiha*.

Soup Chapter

The Soup of Fatima az-Zahra
A story narrated by Hajjah Amina, Cyprus, May 2002

Bismillahi ar-Rahman ar-Rahim

Once Uthman bin Affan invited the Prophet to eat at his house the following day. The Prophet asked Uthman, "Only me, Uthman?" And Uthman replied, "Of course not, Ya Rasul Allah. You along with all of your companions." The Prophet accepted the invitation. The next day the Prophet and his companions began their walk to the house of Uthman. As they walked, the Prophet realized that Uthman was walking behind him. The Prophet asked, "What are you doing?" Uthman replied, "I am counting your steps, Ya Rasul Allah. With each step you take I promise I will free a slave - one step a slave man and one step a slave woman. I will also give 100,000 gold coins as *sadaqa*."

Sayyidina Ali, who had joined the dinner with the Prophet went home that night burdened and sad. His benevolent wife Fatima asked him, "Why are you so upset?" And he told her what Uthman had done, and how he would love to do the same. She said, "Do the same, invite the Prophet tomorrow." Ali replied, "How can we invite him when we are so poor? We don't have enough food." Fatima replied, "Don't worry just invite him, Allah will send us enough food." Ali said, "No, I cannot do such a thing. You are his daughter; you invite him and take the responsibility."
Fatima agreed.

The second day, Ali went to the Prophet and told him that his daughter was inviting him for dinner. The Prophet asked Ali, "Only me, Ali?"

And Ali replied, "Of course not Ya Rasul Allah, all your companions are also welcome." The Prophet ﷺ accepted the invitation. That day, Fatima ؓ began to cook. She took a huge pot and filled it with water. She stirred the water while praying over it. Slowly, Slowly, all different types of food began to fill the pot: meat, vegetables, rice, etc. And the plain water turned into a thick, delicious soup.

The Prophet ﷺ went to his daughter's house, followed by hundreds of his companions. Ali ؓ followed directly behind the Prophet ﷺ, counting his footsteps. When they reached the house of Fatima ؓ, the Prophet ﷺ asked his followers to enter in groups of ten because they were so many for that small house. Ten after ten started to come in and serve themselves from that pot. Up to thirty groups of ten ate from the soup in the pot, and there was still soup left. Fatima ؓ fed her guests, then the neighbors, and most of the village. The pot continued to give more and more food.

When everyone had eaten once, twice, or trice, and Fatima ؓ was sure that everyone had eaten well, she went to her room. There she prayed, she thanked Allah for His Generosity and Mercy. She asked that for every step that the Prophet ﷺ took to her house, Allah would release and save one person from the fires of Hell, one step for a man and one step for a woman. And so it was. *Alhamdulillah*.

Lentil Soup
Shorbat al-'Adas
Middle East

This is a very tasty, rich soup that is high in protein and can be served as a whole meal; delicious on winter nights. Lentil soup is served to the students while in forty-day seclusion, along with bread and olives.

Ingredients
4 cups dried red lentils
Note: These lentils have a bright orangey -red color. They are available at ethnic markets; they are called "*Masoor Dal*" in a Indian stores, or " *'Addas Majroosh*" in Arab stores.
1 cup short grain rice

4 tablespoons olive oil
20 cups water
2 large yellow onions
½ cup corn oil
½ cup lemon juice
4 tablespoons salt

Note: For every 2 cups of lentils, use ½ cup of rice.

<u>Preparation</u>
1. Clean lentils by picking out any debris and rinse.
2. In a soup pot, bring lentils, rice, 1 tablespoon of the olive oil, and water to a boil over high heat.
3. After water comes to a boil, reduce heat to medium and continue cooking, making sure to skim off any foam. Cook until lentils disintegrate and the rice is completely soft.
4. Finely chop onions.
5. In a separate pan, heat corn oil and remaining 3 tablespoons of olive oil. When oil is hot, add chopped onions and cook until dark golden brown, stirring occasionally. Add onions along with any pan drippings to the lentil pot. Add lemon juice and salt. Return to a boil on medium-high heat. Then reduce heat to low and simmer for 5 minutes.
6. Transfer to a serving dish; serve hot.

Serves 8-10

Hajjah Nazihe Adil Kabbani

Creamy Shredded Chicken Soup
Cremali Tawouk Chorbasi
Turkey

Ingredients
2 chicken breasts
4 teaspoons salt
1 teaspoon white pepper
10 cups water
1 egg
12 tablespoons yogurt
1 tablespoon flour
1 cup labne
2 tablespoons butter

Preparation
1. Rinse chicken breasts and cut into strips. Place chicken, salt, and ½ teaspoon of the pepper into a pot; cover with water and bring to a boil.
2. When the chicken is cooked, remove from broth using a slotted spoon and let cool. Shred chicken with your fingers and set aside.
3. Remove the top 7 cups of broth from the pot, leaving behind the broth at the very bottom. Discard the sediment at the bottom of the pot.
4. In a bowl, beat egg and combine with yogurt, flour, lubne and 2 cups of broth. Pour mixture through a sieve back into a clean pot and add the remaining 5 cups of broth. Bring mixture to a boil on high heat. Add shredded chicken and butter to the pot; cook for 2 more minutes.
5. Transfer to a serving dish; serve hot.

Serves 4-6

Meatball and Noodle Soup
Shorbat al-Kafta bi Sha'riyyah
Lebanon

Ingredients
Meatballs:
1 medium onion
1 bunch parsley (1 cup)
1 lb ground beef
2 teaspoons salt
1 teaspoon pepper
1 teaspoon cinnamon
1/2 cup corn oil (for frying)

Broth:
7 tablespoons tomato paste
13 cups water
8 oz bird's nest noodles
5 teaspoons salt
1/2 cup lemon juice
2 teaspoons cinnamon

Preparation
1. Finely chop onion; wash and mince parsley.
2. In a bowl combine onion, parsley, ground beef salt, pepper, and cinnamon. Mix well; let stand for 10 minutes.
3. Use about 1 teaspoon of meat at a time to form meatballs ¾ -inch in diameter.
4. Heat oil in a soup pot at medium high temperature. Add meatballs and sauté until dark brown, turning occasionally to brown evenly; remove meatballs and set aside.
5. Add tomato paste to pot. Pour in the water and bring to a boil. Add bird's nest noodles; break into 1-inch pieces before adding. Add reserved meatballs; stir in salt, lemon juice, and cinnamon.

6. Simmer soup for 15 minutes or until the noodles are tender.
7. Transfer to a serving dish; serve hot.

Serves 6

Tortellini Soup
Pilmeen
Russia

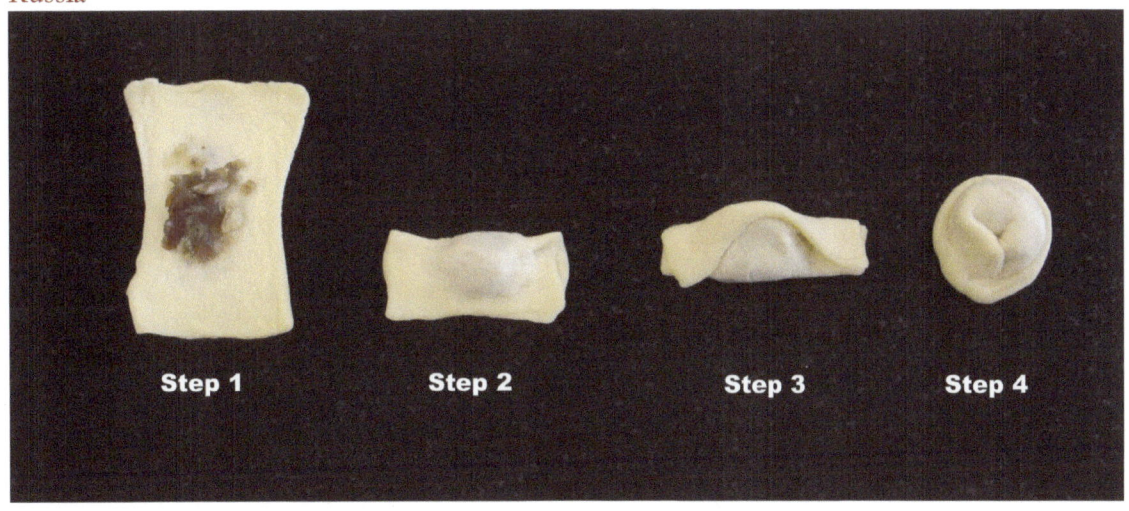

Ingredients
Dough:
1 large egg
1 1/4 cups water
1/2 tsp salt
4 cups flour

Filling:
1 medium onion
1 lb ground beef
2 tsp salt
1 tsp black pepper

Broth:
3 tablespoons butter

1/2 medium onion
5 Tbsp tomato paste
11 cups water
4 small meat or chicken bullion cubes
2 1/2 tsp salt

<u>Preparation</u>
1. To prepare dough, beat together egg, water, and salt.
Note: The egg will help keep dough together.
2. Add 4 cups sifted flour. Knead together with your hands or use a mixer with a dough hook. When the dough holds together and is the consistency of an earlobe, shape into a ball, cover with an overturned bowl, and let rest for 5 minutes.
3. Roll out dough slightly by hand into a log shape. Cut the dough in half; place half back under the covered bowl. Prepare a floured surface and roll out dough to 1/16 inch thickness.
Once the dough is rolled out, use a ruler and make 1¼ inch markings along the side of the dough going up vertically. Use a knife to cut horizontally along these markings, making 1¼ inch thick strips of dough. Make markings at 1¼ inch intervals on each strip of dough. Use a knife to cut along these markings, making 1¼ inch squares. Repeat with other half of dough. Cover dough squares with a towel.
4. To prepare filling finely chop the onion and combine with ground beef; add salt and pepper. Mix well by hand.
5. Uncover half of the dough squares and place ¼ tsp of the meat filling into the center of each square. Then fold each square in half to make a rectangle with a lump of filling in the middle. Press the sides together to seal. Now fold the rectangle in half, bringing the two corners on the right to meet the two corners on the left to form a ring. Press corners to seal. Repeat with other half of dough squares.
6. To prepare broth, melt the butter. Finely chop onion and sauté in the butter until golden and translucent; mix in tomato paste. Add water followed by chicken cubes and salt. Bring to a boil over high heat.
7. Add the peel meen tortellini one at a time; cover and return to a boil. Then reduce heat to medium-low and simmer uncovered for 20 minutes, or until the peel meen float to the top.

8. Transfer to a serving dish; serve warm with yogurt, sumac, and bread.

Serves 4 as a main dish.
Serves 6 as an appetizer.

Brown Lentil and Cumin Soup
Shorbat al-'Adas al-Aswad
Lebanon

This is a great, nourishing soup that Mawlana Shaykh Hisham's mother, Hajjah Yousra, often made during Ramadan. It makes a very nice accompaniment to Fettoush salad.

Ingredients
4 cups brown lentils
¼ cup rice
8 cups water
7 teaspoons salt
8 teaspoons cumin powder
1 medium onion
¼ cup corn oil
½ bunch parsley (½ cup) (garnish)

Preparation
1. Wash the lentils, removing any debris. Add lentils to a pot with enough water to cover by 2 inches. Bring to a boil over high heat; removing any foam that may form. Reduce heat to medium-low and simmer for 20-30 minutes or until tender.
2. Drain lentils by placing a bowl underneath a colander to reserve the liquid. Add drained lentils to a blender or food processor with a very little bit of the liquid. If using the blender, blend in small batches, until smooth. Lentils should become the consistency of a milkshake.
3. Food Mill Method
Transfer lentils, in batches, to a food mill placed over a soup pot. The food mill should catch the lentil skins and let the pulp pass through into the pot. After you have run the lentils through the food mill, remove the lentil skins from the mill to make room for the next batch. After the last batch of lentils is ground, add one cup of water to the mill to remove any remaining lentils.
Strainer Method
Place a fine mesh strainer over a soup pot. Using the back of a spoon, mash the lentils ½

cup at a time into the bottom sides of the strainer. After you have mashed the lentils through the strainer, remove the lentil skins from the strainer to make room for the next batch. After the last batch of lentils is ground, add one cup of water to the mill to remove any remaining lentils.

4. Add 6 cups of the water to the pot along with 6 teaspoons of salt and cumin powder. Add the rice, stirring frequently to prevent rice from sticking to the bottom of the pot. Bring to boil over high heat then reduce heat to medium-low and cook for 15 minutes, or until the rice is tender.

5. Finely chop onion and sauté in corn oil over medium heat until translucent. Add onions and any pan drippings to the soup pot. Bring to a boil over high heat; reduce heat to medium.

6. Mince parsley.

7. Transfer to soup bowls and garnish with parsley; serve hot.

Serves 4-6

Cheese Soup
Shorbah bil-Jibn
Ingredients
1 small onion
2 green peppers
1 stalk celery
2 carrots
¼ cup butter
¼ cup flour
3 ½ cups chicken broth
3 cups shredded cheddar cheese
1 ½ cups milk
1 teaspoon salt
½ teaspoon black pepper
parsley (garnish)

Preparation
1. Chop onion, pepper, celery, and carrots. Melt butter over medium heat in a large pan. Add chopped vegetables and cook for 8 to 10 minutes.
2. After 10 minutes, add flour and stir well.
3. Add chicken broth; mix until thickened.
4. Remove from heat. Add cheese and stir well, until cheese is melted. Add milk, salt, and pepper to taste. Using a hand-held blender puree the soup until smooth. You may also use a food processor or blender; making sure to work in batches.
5. Return to heat and simmer for a few minutes.
6. Ladle hot soup into bowls and garnish with parsley.

Serves 6

Appetizer Chapter

The Eggplant

It is said that when the Prophet ﷺ went on the Isra and Mir'aj, he saw the eggplant under the 'Arsh, the Divine Throne. Thus, the eggplant contains a special energy. When a person eats eggplant with the intention of gaining health he will be given health, Insha-Allah. If a person says, "I'm going to be healed" while eating eggplant, they'll be healed. If a person says, "I'm going to get sick" while eating eggplant, they're going to get sick. The benefit of eating this vegetable depends upon the intention of the person because the eggplant has a powerful energy.

Roasted Eggplant Spread
Baba Ghannouche
Lebanon

Cutting the tops of the bagged eggplants (right)

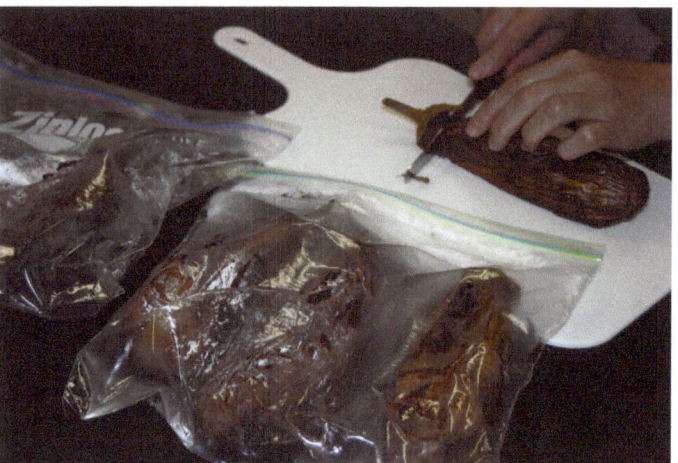

Separating the bitter outer skin of the eggplant (left)

Ingredients
3 large or 6 small eggplants
4 tablespoons tahini (available at Mediterranean markets)
¼ cup lemon juice
4 cloves garlic
2 teaspoons salt
½ teaspoon cumin powder
½ teaspoon paprika
½ bunch parsley (½ cup)
3 teaspoons olive oil

Preparation
1. Preheat oven to 400 F.
2. Bake eggplants uncovered for 1½ hours, turning occasionally until evenly cooked and

soft. Remove from oven; let cool slightly. To separate pulp from the bitter eggplant skins place eggplants in a reseal able bag for at least 15 minutes. Seal the bag. Remove eggplants and cut off the tops 1 inch from the stem. (see picture) One at a time, place eggplants in a resealable bag with the cut part positioned at the mouth of the bag. Squeeze the eggplant from the bottom up into a blender (see picture), discard skin and repeat until all eggplant pulp is in the blender.

Note: If you are using the large variety of eggplant, squeeze pulp into a bowl, separate and discard as many seeds as possible. Transfer pulp to blender.

3. Blend eggplant pulp, tahini, lemon juice, garlic, and salt until thick and smooth.

4. Transfer to a serving dish; sprinkle with cumin and paprika, garnish with parsley and olive oil (see picture). Serve room temperature or chilled.

Serves 4-6

Garbanzo and Tahini Spread
Hummos
Lebanon

Ingredients
2 cups dried garbanzo beans or chickpeas (three 15 oz cans)
1 teaspoon baking soda
¾ cup lemon juice
3 cloves garlic
1 teaspoon salt
½ cup tahini
½ teaspoon cumin powder
½ teaspoon chili powder or paprika
½ bunch parsley (½ cup)
3 teaspoons olive oil

Preparation
1. Place beans, baking soda and enough hot water to cover beans by 2 inches in a large bowl. Let stand overnight; drain and rinse well.
Note: If using canned beans, bring to a boil with fresh water to rid the beans of their tinny taste as well as their gaseous properties; drain and rinse beans well. Bring beans to a boil a second time; remove promptly. Drain and rinse under cold water; reserving 1 cup of liquid. Skip to step 3.
2. Bring beans to a boil over medium high heat in enough fresh water to cover the beans by 3 inches. Simmer for about 1 hour or until tender, making sure to skim off any foam. Drain, reserving 1 cup of liquid.
3. Place the cooked beans in a blender or food processor fitted with the metal blade; blend until smooth. Add reserved water, lemon juice, crushed garlic, salt, and tahini; blend until hummos is the consistency of a paste.
4. Transfer to a shallow serving dish; garnish with cumin, paprika, minced parsley and olive oil. Serve room temperature or chilled.

Hajjah Nazihe Adil Kabbani

Serves 6-8

Garbanzo and Tahini Spread with Ground Beef
Hummos bil-lahm
Lebanon

Ingredients
Hummos (see above)
1 small onion
½ pound ground beef
1 teaspoon salt
½ teaspoon pepper
½ teaspoon cinnamon
2 tablespoons butter
¼ cup pine nuts

Preparation
1. Finely chop onion and brown with ground beef over medium heat. Add salt, pepper and cinnamon.
2. In a saucepan, melt butter; stirring frequently, sauté pine nuts until golden brown. Add sautéed pine nuts and butter to meat mixture and cook together for a couple of minutes.
3. Transfer to a serving dish and garnish prepared hummos with meat mixture. Serve at room temperature.

Serves 6-8

Salad Chapter

Hajjah Naziha: Her Parents' Helper

When Hajjah Naziha was young, she would assist her mother, Her Eminence Hajjah Amina Adil (Allah Ta'ala raise her soul ever higher) in holy service. Tomatoes and cucumbers, zattar and olive oil, cheese and bread, and eggs would be served by Hajjah Amina ق and Hajjah Naziha for the people going on Hajj. They would serve breakfast for the 40-60 people who were going on Hajj with H.E. Mawlana Shaykh Nazim. Before attending the Hajj, the Shaykh and murids would visit many of the holy maqams in Damascus. There they would visit the Ahl el-Bayt, (the family of the Prophet), his daughters and grandchildren and Bilal ☙, and many others, especially Sayyida Zainab ☙. It also includes the Maqam al-Arba'een (the place of the forty living saints), the Ashab al-Kahf (Companions of the Cave), and Mugharat ad-Dem (The Cave of Blood, where Qabil killed Habil).

Everyday Mixed Salad
Salata
Mediterranean

Ingredients
1 medium head Romaine lettuce
1 cucumber
2 medium tomatoes
1 green pepper
½ cup fresh parsley
2 green onions
2 celery sticks (optional)

1 teaspoon salt
¼ cup lemon juice or vinegar
¼ cup olive oil

Preparation
1. Chop the lettuce into ½-inch strips. Peel the cucumber. Dice the cucumber and tomatoes into ¾-inch cubes, and cut the green peppers into 3/4-inch pieces.
2. Mince the parsley. Chop the green onions and celery to ¼-inch pieces.
3. Mix the vegetables in a salad bowl. In a separate bowl, mix the salt, lemon juice (or vinegar), and olive oil. Toss with the vegetables.
4. Serve at room temperature.

Serves 4-6

Crispy Bread and Green Salad in Tangy Garlic Dressing
Fettoush
Lebanon

Ingredients
1 pita bread loaf
1 head Romaine lettuce
2 tomatoes
1 cucumber
2-3 green onions
1/3 bunch parsley (1/3 cup)
1/3 cup olive oil

1/3 cup lemon juice
2 cloves garlic
1/4 teaspoon salt
1 teaspoon sumac
1 tablespoon dried mint

<u>Preparation</u>
1. Cut the pita bread into ¾ inch squares. Toast both sides in the oven under the broiler, or deep fry until golden brown.
Note: The toasted bread resembles croutons. If fried, the bread absorbs the oil making it a heavier, but tastier salad.
2. Finely chop the lettuce and tomatoes. Peel and chop the cucumber. Thinly slice the green onions, and mince the parsley. Combine in a salad bowl.
3. In a separate bowl, mix the olive oil, lemon juice, garlic, salt, sumac, and mint.
4. Just before serving, toss the salad with the dressing and half of the bread. Sprinkle the remaining bread on top. It is important to add the bread just before serving to prevent it from getting soggy.
5. Serve at room temperature.

Serves 4-6

Tomato and Onion Salad
Salatet Benadura
Lebanon

Ingredients
3 large or 9 small tomatoes
1 large onion
4 tablespoons parsley
1 tablespoon salt
¼ cup olive oil

Preparation
1. Finely chop tomatoes and onion; mince parsley.
2. In a bowl, combine tomatoes, onion, parsley, salt, and olive oil; serve at room temperature.

Serves 4-6

Hajjah Nazihe Adil Kabbani

Yogurt and Cucumber Salad
Salatet el-laban bil-khiyyar
Middle East

Ingredients
3 small cucumbers
2 pounds plain yogurt (4 cups)
½ teaspoon salt
1 tablespoon dried mint

Preparation
1. Peel cucumber and chop into ¼ inch cubes; crush mint.
2. In a bowl combine cucumbers, yogurt, salt, and mint; serve chilled.

Serves 4-6

Russian Salad
Russia

Ingredients
Dressing:
6 tablespoons olive oil
2 tablespoons vinegar
¼ teaspoon salt
½ teaspoon black pepper
3 cloves garlic
½ cup mayonnaise

Salad:
1 cup carrot cubes
1 cup potato cubes
1 cup canned or fresh beet cubes
½ cup canned or fresh diced green beans
½ cup frozen peas

Preparation
1. To prepare dressing, combine oil, vinegar, salt, pepper, and garlic in a small bowl. Mix well. Set aside.
2. If using canned beets, drain and chop. If using canned green beans, drain.. Skip to Step 3. If using fresh beets, scrub the beets. Put in a pot with enough water to cover. Bring to a boil over high heat. Reduce the heat to medium, and simmer partially covered for 45 minutes, or until tender. Drain and cool. Peel and cube. If using fresh green beans, wash the beans. Bring water to a boil on high heat. Drop the green beans in and cook for 7 minutes. Drain and cool. Dice into ½-inch pieces.
3. Bring water to a boil on high heat. Add the carrots and potatoes; boil for 7 minutes. Add the peas; boil all together for 2 more minutes. Drain. Add all the vegetables to the dressing. Gently toss to coat with the dressing and set aside for one hour.
3. Drain the dressing and remove the garlic cloves. Add mayonnaise to vegetables; mix well.
4. Transfer to a serving dish. Serve at room temperature or chilled.
Serves 4

Tangy Brown Lentil and Garlic Salad
Salatet el-'adas bil-hamud
Lebanon

Ingredients
1 lb brown lentils (2 cups)
Note: These lentils are widely available. In Arab stores they are known as *"Addas Aswad."*
½ bunch parsley (1/2 cup)
5-6 garlic cloves
1 cup lemon juice
1 cup olive oil
3 teaspoons cumin powder
1 ½ teaspoons salt

1. Soak lentils for 15 minutes with enough water to cover beans by 2 inches; rinse and drain.
2. Bring lentils to a boil over medium high heat in enough water to cover the beans by 3 inches; skimming any foam that forms. Simmer for 15 minutes or until tender as cooking time may vary; drain and rinse immediately with cold water.
3. Mince parsley and crush garlic. In a bowl, combine drained lentils, parsley, garlic, lemon juice, olive oil, cumin and salt.
4. Serve slightly warm or chilled with pita bread, pearl onions and fresh mint leaves.

Serves 4-6

Tangy White Bean and Onion Salad
Fasulye Sachta
Cyprus

Ingredients
1½ lbs white beans (24 oz)
1 tablespoon baking soda
½ bunch parsley (1/2 cup)
1 medium onion

Hajjah Nazihe Adil Kabbani

½ cup lemon juice
1 cup olive oil
2 teaspoons salt

<u>Preparation</u>
1. Place beans, baking soda and enough water to cover beans by 2 inches in a large bowl. Let stand overnight; drain and rinse well.
2. Bring beans to a boil over medium high heat in enough water to cover the beans by 3 inches. Simmer for 15-30 minutes or until tender, making sure to skim off any foam. Drain and rinse with cold water.
3. Mince parsley and chop onion. In a bowl combine with beans, parsley, onion, lemon juice, olive oil and salt in a bowl; serve at room temperature.

Serves 4-6

Bean Chapter

The Blessings of Guests

"*Ad-Daif Daifullah*," is a traditional Arabic saying, which means, "Guests are the guests of Allah ﷻ." This elevates hosting to a Divinely-given responsibility.

Hosting is also a source of Divinely-given blessings. H.E. Mawlana Shaykh Nazim never eats without guests. Guests come with their own *rizq* (provisions), their own blessing. Thus, anyone who hosts a guest in their house will have *baraka* (blessings) in their house for the next forty days. There will be blessings in both the provisions and food of the host. H.E. Shaykh Nazim's wife, H.E. Hajjah Amina, would say, "How could Allah ﷻ not give us many blessings? We always have so many guests."

Hajjah Nazihe Adil Kabbani

Cumin Seasoned Old World Lentils
M'Jaddarah
Lebanon

Ingredients
1 medium onion
½ cup corn oil
¼ cup olive oil
8¼ cups water
4 cups red lentils

Note: These lentils have a bright orange/red color. They are available at ethnic markets; called "*Masoor Dal*" in a Indian stores, or " '*Addas Majroosh*" in Arab stores.
½ cup short-grain rice
5 teaspoons salt
cumin powder (garnish)

Preparation
1. Finely chop onion.
2. Heat corn oil and olive oil in a large pot; add onion and sauté until dark brown.
Note: The onion is blackened to give a rich taste and dark color to the broth.
3. Add 8 cups of water and bring to a boil over medium high heat. Boil for five minutes, or until the water turns a very dark color. This is to make a broth which absorbs the color and flavor of the blackened onions. Remove and strain broth through a fine mesh strainer into a

bowl to remove the onion pieces. See picture.

4. Return broth to pot. Rinse lentils. Rinse rice. Add lentils, rice, and salt. Cover pot and bring to a boil again on high heat. Uncover the pot. Reduce the heat to low and simmer, stirring constantly, for 20-30 minutes, until mixture is the consistency of a thick paste.

Note: If mixture sticks to pan or rice is not yet tender, gradually add cold water ¼ cup at a time. This prevents a thin or runny end result.

5. Transfer to a serving dish and garnish with cumin.

6. Serve at room temperature.

Serves 4-6

White Beans and Carrots
Zeytinyağlı Quru Fasulye
Turkey

From Hajjah Nazihe's Aunt Zahra; Hajjah Nazihe's Father, H.E. Mawlana Shaykh Nazim's sister, Zahra.

Hajjah Nazihe Adil Kabbani

Ingredients:
1½ lbs dried white beans (24 oz)
1 teaspoon baking soda
1/4 cup corn oil
1/2 cup olive oil
1 medium-sized onion
5 carrots
1 tablespoon tomato paste
4 teaspoons salt
¼ teaspoon sugar
3 cups water
¼ cup parsley (garnish)
lemon juice (garnish)

Preparation
1. Place beans, baking soda and enough hot water to cover beans by 2 inches in a large bowl. Let stand overnight; drain and rinse well.
2. Bring beans to a boil over medium high heat in enough fresh water to cover the beans by 3 inches. Reduce heat to medium and cook until tender, approximately 30 minutes; making sure to skim off any foam that may form. Be careful not to overcook or the beans will be mushy. Rinse cooked beans in a colander under cold water and set aside.
3. Mince onions; peel and slice carrots into thin rounds. Heat corn oil and olive oil in a deep pot at a high temperature, Sauté minced onions until soft and yellow, but not brown. Add carrots and cook approximately five minutes until carrots are soft; gently stir in beans.
4. In a bowl, combine tomato paste, salt, and sugar with three cups of water; pour mixture into bean pot.
5. Cook uncovered on medium-low heat for 10 minutes, gently stirring until water evaporates. Beans should be soft, but still hold their shape.
6. When the mixture has thickened and liquid has evaporated remove from heat.
7. Transfer to a serving dish and garnish with parsley; drizzle with lemon juice. The lemon juice adds a particularly nice flavor to this dish.
8. Serve at room temperature with pita bread.

Vegetable Sides Chapter

The Purity of Hajjah Naziha

Hajjah Naziha said, "When I was 12, my mother had a very difficult delivery with my sister. My father took me outside and gave me the Qur'an and told me to read Surat al-Balad on some water to help her. My mother drank the water and delivered my sister after half an hour."

Mawlana Shaykh Hisham explained that H.E. Mawlana Shaykh Nazim had Hajjah Naziha read it because of her youth and piety. She read this surat before she had reached the age of maturity. If the one reading has no sin they have nothing written on their left side. Purity gives a greater chance for effectiveness. Because of these attributes she used to write the *tawiz* for Grandshaykh at this age.

Leeks and Tomatoes
Domatesli Pırasa
Turkey

Ingredients
2 lbs leeks (about 3 leeks)
1 large tomato
¼ cup corn oil
¼ cup olive oil
1 teaspoon salt

Preparation
1. To prepare leeks, one at a time cut off the bulb and dry ends; remove the outer layers. Cut leeks lengthwise down the center; slice the white end of the leeks into ¼ inch semicircles.
2. Keeping the white and green portion of leeks separate, place the white portion of cut leeks into a bowl; fill with water. Slice the green end of leeks, place the green portion of cut leeks into a bowl; fill with water. Soak for at least 15 minutes. While soaking, separate leek layers with your fingers to loosen any dirt.
3. Meanwhile, chop tomato.
4. Lift leeks out of the water leaving behind any loose dirt that has settled at the bottom of the bowls. Rinse leeks in a colander making sure to keep the white and green sections

separate.
5. Add corn oil and olive oil to a pan over medium heat. Once the oil is hot, add the white part of the leeks and sauté until tender (see picture). Add tomatoes and salt; sauté for a couple of minutes. Add the green leek sections; cover and simmer until tender.
8. Serve warm or cool.

Serves 4-6

Fried Okra and Tomatoes
Domatesli Bamya
Turkey

Ingredients
4 lbs whole okra, fresh or frozen
corn oil (for frying)
3 teaspoons salt
1 large white onion
2 large tomatoes
¾ cup to 1½ cups corn oil
2 teaspoons salt
1 teaspoon black pepper
½ cup lemon juice

Preparation
1. Preheat oven to 350F.
2. If using fresh okra, cut the end off to look like a cone hat.
3. Heat the oil, and add 1 teaspoon of salt to the oil. When the oil is hot, add the okra; fry until okra is light golden.
Note: Okra will seem to be a lighter color in the oil than when you remove it. The fried okra should be dark green.
4. Remove okra with a slotted spoon and place in a colander; set aside.
Note: Avoid overcooking okra as it will become too dark and the pod will open.
5. Finely chop onion and tomatoes.
6. In a saucepan, heat ¾ cup corn oil (you can either reuse the frying oil or use fresh oil). When the oil is hot, add the onions and sauté until soft and yellow. Reduce the heat to medium. Add 2 teaspoons of salt along with tomatoes; sauté until soft. Add pepper and lemon juice; set aside.
7. Place fried okra in a baking dish. Evenly spread the onion-tomato mixture over the okra. Dissolve 1 teaspoon of salt in a cup of water; pour saltwater into the baking dish.
8. Bake covered for 30 minutes; serve. Serve at room temperature.

Serves 4-6

Hajjah Nazihe Adil Kabbani

Stuffed Green Peppers with Coriander Seeds and Garlic
Fleifle Mahshiyya
Lebanon

Ingredients
2 lbs green bell peppers*
1 cup corn oil
2 teaspoons salt (or to taste)
1 lb very soft tomatoes
5 tablespoons coriander seeds
1 head garlic
 *For best results, use small, round peppers of similar size.

<u>Preparation</u>
1. Pre heat oven to 350°F.
2. Wash and dry the peppers. Cut a circle around the stems and separate from the tops of the peppers. Remove the seeds and white part from inside the peppers.
3. Heat the oil in a frying pan over medium-high heat. Stir a teaspoon of salt into the oil to prevent it from splattering. When the oil is hot, fry the peppers, continuously turning until an even, golden color. .
4. Meanwhile, peel the tomatoes, take the skin off and chop them into ½ inch cubes. Crush garlic cloves.
5. Warm 6 tablespoons of oil from the peppers in a pan over low heat. Fry the crushed garlic and 1 teaspoon of the salt. Once the garlic has turned a golden color, add 5 tablespoons of coriander seeds and fry for another 2 minutes; set aside.
6. Place green peppers side by side in a 13x9x2 inch Pyrex dish. Evenly distribute the garlic and coriander mixture among the green peppers, putting some of the mixture inside the green peppers just to add some flavor.
7. Add chopped tomatoes around the peppers in the pan. Add ½ cup of water in the pan; making sure not to add water inside the peppers themselves. Sprinkle 1 teaspoon of salt over the tomatoes.
8. Cover the dish with foil and place in the preheated oven until sauce comes to a boil; simmer between 15-25 minutes. Remove from oven and serve at room temperature or refrigerate and serve cold.

Serves 4-6

Carrots, Brussel Sprouts, and Broccoli
Zeytinyağla Bruxel Lahanna-si
Turkey

<u>Ingredients</u>
2 carrots
3 lbs Brussels sprouts
2 teaspoons salt
½ lb frozen broccoli florets
¼ cup corn oil
¼ cup olive oil
1 medium onion
5 plum tomatoes
1 teaspoon pepper
1 teaspoon cumin powder

Preparation
1. Peel the carrots and slice into ¼-inch rounds.
2. Cut off the base of the Brussels sprouts, remove outer layer of leaves, and cut an "X" in the base.
3. Add Brussels sprouts, 1 teaspoon salt, and enough water to cover Brussels sprouts by 2 inches; bring to a boil on high heat. Reduce heat to medium and cook until tender; drain and rinse.
4. Add broccoli florets to a pot with enough water to cover by 2 inches; bring to a boil on high heat. Reduce heat to medium and cook until tender; drain and rinse.
5. Finely chop onion. Heat corn and olive oil in a large pot, Sauté onion until translucent, add carrots and sauté for five more minutes.
6. With a cheese grater, grate tomatoes to remove outer skin. Add tomato pulp to the onion and carrot mixture; sauté together for a couple of minutes. Add Brussels sprouts and broccoli; cover and simmer over low heat.
7. Meanwhile, dissolve 1 teaspoon each of the salt, pepper, and cumin in one cup of water; stir well and add to the pot. Simmer while covered over low heat for five minutes.
8. Serve at room temperature.

Serves 4-6

Zucchini with Yogurt Sauce
Yoğurtlu Kabak
Turkey

Ingredients
2 lbs zucchini
corn oil (for frying)
1½ teaspoons salt
3 garlic cloves
3 cups plain yogurt

Preparation
1. Slice zucchini into ¼ inch rounds. Place zucchini in the sun to dry or place on paper towels for 15 minutes; turning them over to make sure both sides dry evenly.
2. Sprinkle zucchini with a pinch of salt on each side.
Note: The salt prevents excessive oil absorption during frying.
3. Heat corn oil at a high temperature. Stir ½ teaspoon of the salt into the oil. When the oil is hot, add zucchini and fry until dark golden brown; turning occasionally to cook evenly on both sides.
4. Remove zucchini from oil with a slotted spoon and drain on a plate lined with paper towels.
5. Crush the garlic and in a separate bowl, combine yogurt, garlic, and remaining salt.
6. Transfer zucchini to a serving dish, cover with yogurt sauce; serve at room temperature.

Serves 4-6

Eggplant with Yogurt and Garlic
Beyttenjan Mukli bil-Laban
Mediterranean

Ingredients
3 large eggplants
2 tablespoons plus 2 teaspoons salt
3 cups plain yogurt
4 garlic cloves
2 cups corn oil (for frying)

Preparation
1. Peel the eggplants lengthwise, leaving on some skin in a zebra stripe pattern. Slice into ½ inch thick rounds; place rounds in a bowl and sprinkle evenly with 2 tablespoons of salt. Let stand for half an hour.
Note: The salt prevents the eggplant form absorbing too much oil while frying and draws out the eggplant's bitter juices.
2. Meanwhile, crush the garlic cloves. To prepare the yogurt sauce combine yogurt, crushed garlic, and 1 teaspoon of the salt in a bowl; refrigerate.
3. Take each eggplant round and squeeze in your fist to remove bitter juices.

4. Warm corn oil on high heat; stir in 1 teaspoon of salt. Once oil is hot, add eggplant rounds and fry for about 4 minutes on each side. Repeat in batches until all eggplant rounds are fried.
5. Transfer the fried eggplant rounds to a long serving dish; top evenly with the chilled yogurt sauce.
6. Serve cold.

Serves 4-6

Portuguese Potatoes
Mediterranean

Ingredients
10 medium potatoes
3 tablespoons parsley
3 tablespoons olive oil
1 teaspoon salt

Preparation
1. Peel the potatoes and cut in half lengthwise. Then cut across each half into 1 inch slices. Bring the potatoes to a boil on high heat in enough water to cover by 2 inches; reduce heat to medium and boil until barely tender. You should be able to put a fork in them, but not easily. Drain and rinse with cold water.
2. Preheat oven to 400F.
3. Place potatoes into a baking dish. Mince the parsley. Add parsley, olive oil and salt to baking dish; toss gently with potatoes; bake for 15-20 minutes, or until the top is golden brown.
4. Serve with Kafta. Serve hot. This is an especially child-friendly dish.

Serves 6-8

Home Style French Fries
Battata Maqlia
Mediterranean

Ingredients
8 large potatoes
2 ½ cups corn oil (for frying)
Salt to taste

Preparation
1. Peel and wash potatoes. First slice potatoes lengthwise into thick ovals. Then slice the ovals lengthwise to 1/3 inch thick or desired thickness (to the size of a finger).
2. Let the potatoes sit in cold water until oil is hot or fry directly after cutting if you are in a hurry. If soaking in water, drain in colander several minutes before frying.
3. Heat the oil on medium high heat and add ½ teaspoon of salt to avoid splattering. Add a handful of the cut potatoes at a time (so they do not stick together). Fry in batches so that the oil covers the potatoes. Fry until golden brown.
Note: A deep fryer can be used or a stock pot.
4. Remove with a slotted spoon to a platter covered with paper towels. Sprinkle with salt while still hot. Continue until all the potatoes are fried.
5. Serve hot.

Serves 4-5

This makes a child-friendly snack or side dish.

Rice Chapter

The Stingy Man and the Generous Man

Allah ﷻ told Sayyidina Musa ﷺ, "There are two people. One person is going to Hell, and one is going to Paradise." Sayyidina Musa ﷺ went to see the people. The first man fasted excessively, and had a stream by him and a pomegranate tree. For breakfast in the day, he would drink water from the stream. In the evening, he would eat the fruit from the tree. He would get two pomegranates. But when he saw Sayyidina Musa ﷺ come, the man hid one of the pomegranates, so he would only have to share one. He ate half the pomegranate, and gave the other half to Sayyidina Musa ﷺ. This man was stingy. Stinginess is from Shaytan's attributes so this man was destined for hellfire.

Then Sayyidina Musa ﷺ went to see the other man, who was very generous. However he made his living by attacking the caravans that passed him, stealing their goods and camels. He gave Sayyidina Musa ﷺ the best that he had of everything from his choicest provisions. This man was generous. Generosity is one of Allah's attributes so this man was destined for Paradise.

Leeks with Rice and Carrots
Pırınçli Zeytinyağlı Pırasa
Turkey

Ingredients
2 lbs leeks
2 large carrots
1 medium onion
1 tomato
1 cup short-grain rice
3 tablespoons salt
1 tablespoon + 2 teaspoons sugar
2 ½ cups water
¾ cup olive oil

Preparation

1. To prepare leeks, cut off ends and remove outer layers. Chop into 1 inch wide pieces.
2. Finely chop onion; peel and slice carrots into 1/8 inch rounds. Warm olive oil in a cooking pot over medium heat; add onion and sauté until tender and yellow.
3. Cut tomato in half and hold by the skin; grate until you are left with just the outside skin of the tomato. Discard skin and add tomato pulp to pot; simmer for 2 minutes.
4. Rinse rice in cold water a few times until the water runs clear; drain and set aside.
5. Add leeks, carrots, rice, salt, sugar, and water. Stirring occasionally, cook covered on high heat for about 15 minutes or until leeks are tender and rice is cooked.
6. Transfer to a dish and serve chilled.

Serves 4

Rice Pilaf with Meat Chunks and Carrots
Bukhari Pilav
Uzbekistan

Ingredients
Meat and Broth:
1 onion
2 lbs lamb chunks, with or without bones
2 tablespoons salt
1 tablespoon pepper
1 tablespoon cinnamon
2 bay leaves
10 cups water

Rice:
3 onions
1 ½ lbs carrots
1 ½ sticks butter or 1 cup corn oil
8 tablespoons tomato paste
4 cups rice, either Basmati or medium-grain
2 tablespoons salt
4 teaspoons pepper
3 teaspoons cinnamon

Preparation
1. Chop onion. Add onion, meat, salt, pepper, cinnamon, and bay leaves to a pressure cooker or soup pot with 10 cups of water.

Pressure Cooker Method:
Close lid and cook on high heat until mixture comes to a boil. Reduce heat to medium and cook for 45 minutes, or until the meat is tender.

Soup Pot Method:
Cook on high until mixture comes to a boil. Reduce heat to medium and simmer for one and a half hours, or until the meat is tender. When you reduce heat to simmer adjust the lid so the pot is partially uncovered to prevent boiling over.

Rice Preparation:
1. Finely chop 2 onions; peel and shred carrots. Melt butter in a pot; add onions and carrots. Cook on medium heat, stirring occasionally. After 5 minutes, reduce heat to medium low and cook until carrots are soft and tender. Stir in tomato paste.
2. Remove meat mixture from the pot with a slotted spoon; leaving the covered meat broth to simmer over low heat. Taste meat broth to adjust seasoning.
3. Add the meat mixture along with salt, 3 teaspoons pepper, and 2 teaspoons cinnamon to the onions and carrots.
4. Rinse rice in cold water a few times until the water runs clear; drain. Place rice directly on

top of the carrot-meat mixture. Do not stir, simply let rice rest on top of the mixture.
5. Slowly add 8 cups of meat broth pouring from one spot on the rim of the pot. Cover and cook on medium heat until rice has absorbed most of the liquid. Reduce heat to low and simmer for ten more minutes or until rice is soft and all liquid is absorbed.
6. Wrap the pot lid with a towel and replace to steam the rice for five to ten minutes.
7. Transfer mixture to a serving platter; first form a bed of rice, then decorate with meat mixture on top.
8. Serve hot with yogurt or yogurt-cucumber salad

Serves 10-12

Perfect Rice Pilaf
Turkey

Ingredients
2 cups rice
1 teaspoon salt
¼ teaspoon ground black pepper
2 onions
2 cups shredded carrot
4 tablespoons olive oil
2 chicken bullion cubes
3 cups water

Preparation
1. Rinse rice thoroughly and in a bowl cover rice with water by 2 inches. Allow to soak for 30 minutes; drain. Add salt and pepper to uncooked rice.
2. Finely chop onion and shred carrots.
3. In a medium pot, sauté onion in olive oil over medium heat until lightly browned. Add carrots and sauté for another 5 minutes. Add chicken bullions and water; making sure to dissolve the bullions completely. Bring to a boil over medium-high heat; add rice and bring back to a boil.
4. Cover pot and cook over medium-low heat for 20-25 minutes, until water is absorbed and knife inserted into bottom of rice is comes out dry.
5. Remove from heat. Line pot lid with a paper towel and allow rice to sit another 10-15 minutes before serving. Serve hot.

Serves 8

Savory Pastry Chapter

The Salt and Sayyidina Ibrahim

After Sayyidina Ibrahim ﷺ built the Ka'ba, he said, "Oh, Allah, I built your House. Who is going to visit this house in the dessert?"

Allah ﷻ revealed to him, "People will come." And then Sayyidina Ibrahim ﷺ heard many voices saying, "*Labbayk, Allahuma Labayk*" "At your service, Allah." Because Sayyidina Ibrahim was very generous and hospitable he became worried. He heard the sounds of millions of people saying, "*Labbayk*," and thought, "How am I going to feed all these people in the dessert?"

Angel Gabriel ﷺ came with 1 glass of water from Paradise. Angel Gabriel ﷺ said, "Don't be confused. These are the voices of your descendants, that will be coming until Judgment Day to visit this House." He threw the water. The wind blew half of the water into the mountains and the other half into the rivers. This water became salt. That is why you find rock salt and ocean salt.

The salt came after Sayyidina Ibrahim ﷺ threw the water in the rivers and mountains. From the hospitality of Sayyidina Ibrahim ﷺ, Allah Ta'ala created salt. The salt gives a nice taste to the food. Until this day all humans benefit from the generosity of Sayyidina Ibrahim ﷺ.

Hajjah Nazihe Adil Kabbani

Ground Beef Pastry Squares
Sfiha ba'al-bakkia
Lebanon

<u>Ingredients</u>
Dough:
4 ¼ cups flour
½ teaspoon baking soda
1 teaspoon salt
½ cup water
¼ cup corn oil

1 cup yogurt

Filling:
1 medium onion
3 medium tomatoes
1 lb ground beef
1 ½ teaspoons salt
1 teaspoon pepper
1 teaspoon cinnamon
2 teaspoons chili sauce (optional)
1 tablespoon pomegranate juice (optional)
2 tablespoons butter
¼ cup pine nuts

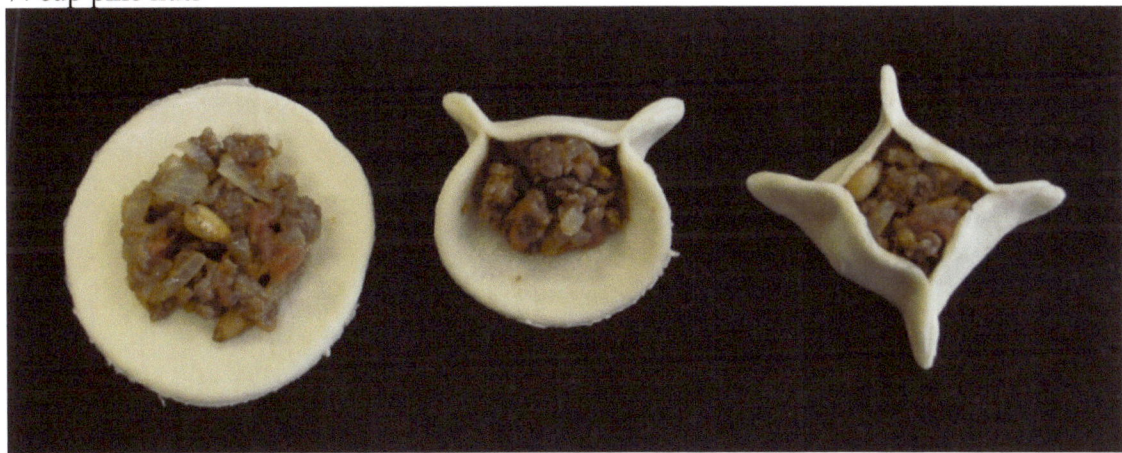

Preparation
1. To prepare dough, combine flour, baking soda, and salt in a bowl. In a separate bowl, combine water, oil, and yogurt. To prevent any lumps from forming, gradually incorporate the dry ingredients into wet ingredients.
2. Knead dough by hand, or use a mixer with a dough hook, until it becomes the consistency of an earlobe. If the dough is too soft or sticky, add more flour. If the dough is too stiff or hard, add water by dampening hands and working into dough.

3. Divide dough into 2 equal halves. Knead and form each half into a ball; place the two halves in a bowl and cover bowl with a slightly damp towel. The dough should rest for at least 30 minutes.

4. To prepare filling, finely chop onion; peel, and cube tomatoes. Brown ground beef and onion on medium-low heat, continuously working the meat with a wooden spoon to achieve a crumbly texture. Simmer long enough to allow the beef to absorb all liquid in pan; add the tomatoes and cook a few more minutes. Add salt, pepper, cinnamon, chili sauce, and pomegranate juice.

5. Separately, sauté the pine nuts in melted butter on medium heat until golden brown. Add pine nuts and any pan drippings to beef mixture; sauté for a few minutes on low heat, remove from heat, and let cool.

6. Preheat oven to 400°F.

7. To roll out dough, prepare a floured surface. Remove the first half of dough from the covered bowl and knead long enough to eliminate any air pockets or creases. Use a rolling pin and roll out dough to the thickness of an earlobe, about 1/8 inch thick.

8. Use a wide-mouthed coffee cup to cut out as many circles as possible from the rolled out dough; cover with a towel. To fill pastries, place between ½-2/3 of a tablespoon of the meat mixture in the center of each circle. To shape dough into squares, pinch the edges of the circular dough together in 4 evenly spaced places about ¼ inch in from the rim of the circle. This should form an open-faced square with oval shaped pockets at each corner. The filling should be showing in the middle of the square.

9. Lightly grease a baking sheet with olive oil; transfer open-faced squares onto baking sheet. Place in the middle rack of a preheated oven and cook for 15-25 minutes, until pastry edges are golden brown. Repeat process with other half of dough.

10. Serve hot or at room temperature.

Makes 20-25 small meat pies, each measuring about 2 ½ inches square.

Pastry squares can be served as an appetizer for a party, a side dish at dinner, or a main dish for 4-5 people.

Heavenly Foods

Triangle Spinach Pies
Fatayir bi-Sbanekh
Lebanon

Hajjah Nazihe Adil Kabbani

<u>Ingredients</u>
Dough:
4 ¼ cups flour
½ teaspoon baking soda
1 teaspoon salt
½ cup water
¼ cup corn oil
1 cup yogurt
Filling:
1 large onion
20 oz chopped frozen spinach
½ cup corn oil
½ cup lemon juice
2 teaspoons salt
1 tablespoon sumac
½ teaspoon cinnamon
1 teaspoon chili powder (optional)
1 tablespoon pomegranate juice (optional)

Preparation
1. To prepare dough, combine flour, baking soda, and salt in a bowl. In a separate bowl, combine water, oil, and yogurt. To prevent any lumps from forming, gradually incorporate the dry ingredients into the wet ingredients.
2. Knead dough by hand, or use a mixer with a dough hook, until it becomes the consistency of an earlobe. If the dough is too soft or sticky, add more flour. If the dough is too stiff or hard, add water by dampening hands and working into dough.
3. Divide dough into 2 equal halves. Knead and form each half into a ball; place the two halves in a
bowl and cover bowl with a slightly damp towel. The dough should rest for at least 30 minutes.
4. To prepare filling, finely chop onion, thaw spinach and squeeze out excess water.
Note: If the filling is too "juicy" it will leak out of the dough.
5. Over medium heat, sauté onions in oil until light golden brown. Add spinach and sauté together for two minutes; reduce heat to low. Add lemon juice, salt, sumac, cinnamon, chili powder, and pomegranate juice. Cook for an additional 2-3 minutes. Remove filling from heat and let cool.
6. Preheat oven to 400°F.

7. To roll out dough, prepare a floured surface. Divide dough into four equal pieces. Leave the four equal pieces underneath an overturned bowl to keep from drying out. Remove the first section of dough out of the bowl and knead long enough to eliminate any air pockets or creases. Use a rolling pin and roll out dough to the thickness of an earlobe, about 1/8 inch thick.

8. Use a wide coffee cup turned upside-down to make circles in the dough. Cut as many circles as possible from the flattened dough. Put half 1 tablespoon of the filling in the center of each circle of dough. Keep the remaining circles of dough covered with a
towel to keep them from drying out. The spinach pies should be shaped into triangles; in 3 lines like a pyramid with the seam showing on top. To shape into triangles, bring the right and left side of the circle to meet in the center; pinch firmly to seal. Then bring the bottom of the circle up to the sides and again pinch firmly to seal. It is important to seal tightly so the pastries will not open in the baking process.

Note: If the ends of the dough do not seal properly, or get dried out, use a little water on your hands to help seal them.

9.   The filling should not be visible once the top is closed. If it is too juicy to close, reduce the filling amount.

10.   Place the sealed pies on an oiled baking sheet and repeat until the first baking sheet is full. Place in the preheated oven and bake for 10-15 minutes, until the dough is lightly golden.

11. Repeat the process with remaining dough and filling.

12. Transfer to a serving dish.   Serve hot or at room temperature.

Makes approximately 35 small triangular spinach pies, each measuring about 2 ½ inches. Pastry triangles can be served as an appetizer for a party, a side dish at dinner, or a main dish for 4-5 people.

Heavenly Foods

Hajjah Nazihe Adil Kabbani

Cheese-Filled Pastry Squares
Peynirli Börek
Cyprus

Heavenly Foods

Hajjah Nazihe Adil Kabbani

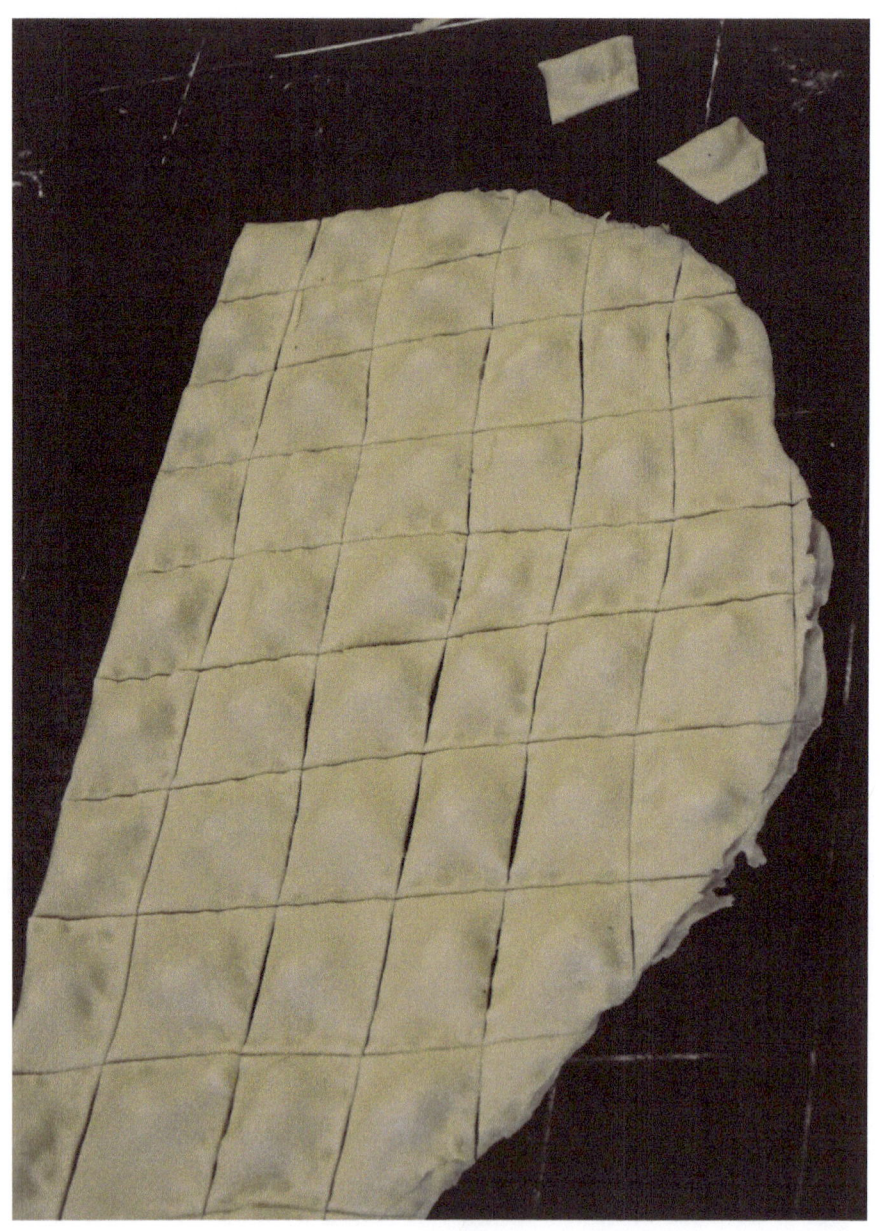

Ingredients
Dough:
1 cup water
¼ cup corn oil
¼ teaspoon salt
3 ¼ cups flour

Filling:
16 oz mild feta cheese
½ bunch parsley (½ cup)
2 eggs
oil (for frying)

Preparation
1. Mix water, oil, and salt. Add the flour a little at a time. If the dough is too soft or sticky, add more flour. If the dough is too stiff or hard, add water by dampening hands and working into dough. Knead dough by hand, or use a mixer with a dough hook, until it forms a large ball a little bit tougher than the consistency of an earlobe; set aside in a bowl covered with a damp towel.
2. To prepare filling, grate cheese, mince parsley, and beat egg; combine and set aside.
3. To roll out dough, prepare a floured surface. Divide dough into five equal portions. Take the first section of dough out of covered bowl and knead long enough to eliminate any air pockets or creases. Use a rolling pin, roll out dough to the thickness of a milk carton, about 1/16 inch thick; almost as thin as phyllo dough.
4. Starting in the middle of the dough, place a teaspoon of cheese filling about 1 inch away from the edge. Repeat, spacing 1-inch apart to form a straight line. Continue making rows one above the other until half of the dough is covered with the cheese filling. There should be a 1 inch border around the entire edge of the dough that is uncovered. Fold the remaining half of the dough over the filled half and press firmly with your fingertips around each mound of filling, forming square shapes (see photo).
5. Cut along the edges of the pressed squares with a pizza cutter, a pastry cutting wheel, or the edge of a Turkish coffee or espresso plate until the square is separated from the rest of

the dough. The uncooked pastries should measure 2 to 2 ½ inches square. Repeat process with remaining dough and filling.

6. Warm corn oil to 350°F in a pan over high heat. The pastry squares should be immersed in enough oil to cover by 2-3 inches. Drop a small piece of dough into the oil. If the dough rises, the oil is ready for frying. Add 6-7 pastries at a time to the hot oil and fry until lightly golden. Cook for 1 minute on each side, turning once to ensure even cooking. As each batch is finished, transfer to a plate lined with paper towels to drain any excess oil. Store fried pastries, uncovered, in a warm oven (approximately 170°F) until ready to serve. Continue frying until all the pastries are done. Pastries should be puffed and tender.
Note: If the pastries are oily, the heat of the oil is not high enough and should be increased.
7. Transfer to a platter. Serve hot or at room temperature.

Makes approximately 60 small cheese pastries, each measuring about 2 ½ inches square. These are often served with tea. This can be served as an appetizer for a party, a side dish at dinner, or a main dish for 4-5 people.

Golden Half-Moon Beef Pastries
Etli Börek
Cyprus

Ingredients
1 cup water
¼ cup corn oil
¼ teaspoon salt
3 ¼ cups flour

Filling:
1 medium onion
¼ bunch parsley
1 ½ lbs ground beef or lamb
2 teaspoons salt
1 teaspoon pepper
1 teaspoon cinnamon

Preparation
1. . Mix water, oil, and salt. Add the flour a little at a time. If the dough is too soft or sticky, add more flour. If the dough is too stiff or hard, add water by dampening hands and working into dough. Knead dough by hand, or use a mixer with a dough hook, until it forms a large ball a little bit tougher than the consistency of an earlobe; set aside in a bowl covered with a damp towel.
2. To prepare the filling, finely chop the onion and mince the parsley. Brown the ground beef and onion over medium heat, continuously working the meat with a wooden spoon to achieve a crumbly texture. Once the beef releases and reabsorbs its juices, add parsley, salt, pepper, and cinnamon; mix well. Remove from heat and set aside to cool.
3. Knead the dough slightly and separate into five equal portions. Work one portion at a time, leaving the remaining portions under an overturned bowl.
4. To roll out dough, prepare a floured surface. With a rolling pin, roll out the dough to the thickness of a milk carton (approximately 1/16-inch thick). It will be almost as thin as

phyllo dough and oval-shaped.

5. Spoon 1 ½ teaspoons of filling to one edge of the dough in a straight line, leaving about 2 inches of unfilled border around the perimeter of the dough. Each 1 ½ teaspoons of filling should be spaced about 2-2 ½ inches apart and lined up in a row.

6. Pick up the edges of the dough gently folding the dough over the row with the meat filling. Fold the remaining half of the dough over the filled half and press firmly with your fingertips around each mound of filling (see photo).

7. Gently press down with your thumb in a crescent shape on the opposite side of the folded edge around each pile of meat filling.

8. Cut over the edge of the thumb trail with a cutting wheel, or Turkish coffee plate until the meat pie crescent is separated from the rest of the dough. Continue until all of the dough is shaped into half-moons or crescents.

9. Repeat the same method with the remaining four pieces of dough.

10. Warm corn oil to 350°F in a pan over high heat. The pastries should be immersed in enough oil to cover by 2-3 inches. . Drop a small piece of dough into the oil. If the dough rises, the oil is ready for frying. Add 6-7 pastries at a time to the hot oil and fry until lightly golden. Cook for 1 minute on each side, turning once to ensure even cooking. As each batch is finished, transfer to a plate lined with paper towels to drain any excess oil. Store fried pastries, uncovered, in a warm oven (approximately 170°F) until ready to serve. Continue frying until all the pastries are done. Pastries should be puffed and tender.

Note: If the pastries are oily, the heat of the oil is not high enough and should be increased.

11. Transfer to a platter. Serve hot or at room temperature.

Heavenly Foods

Savory Rice with Beef and Nuts Enveloped in Phyllo Pastry
Ouzi
Syria

Hajjah Nazihe Adil Kabbani

Heavenly Foods

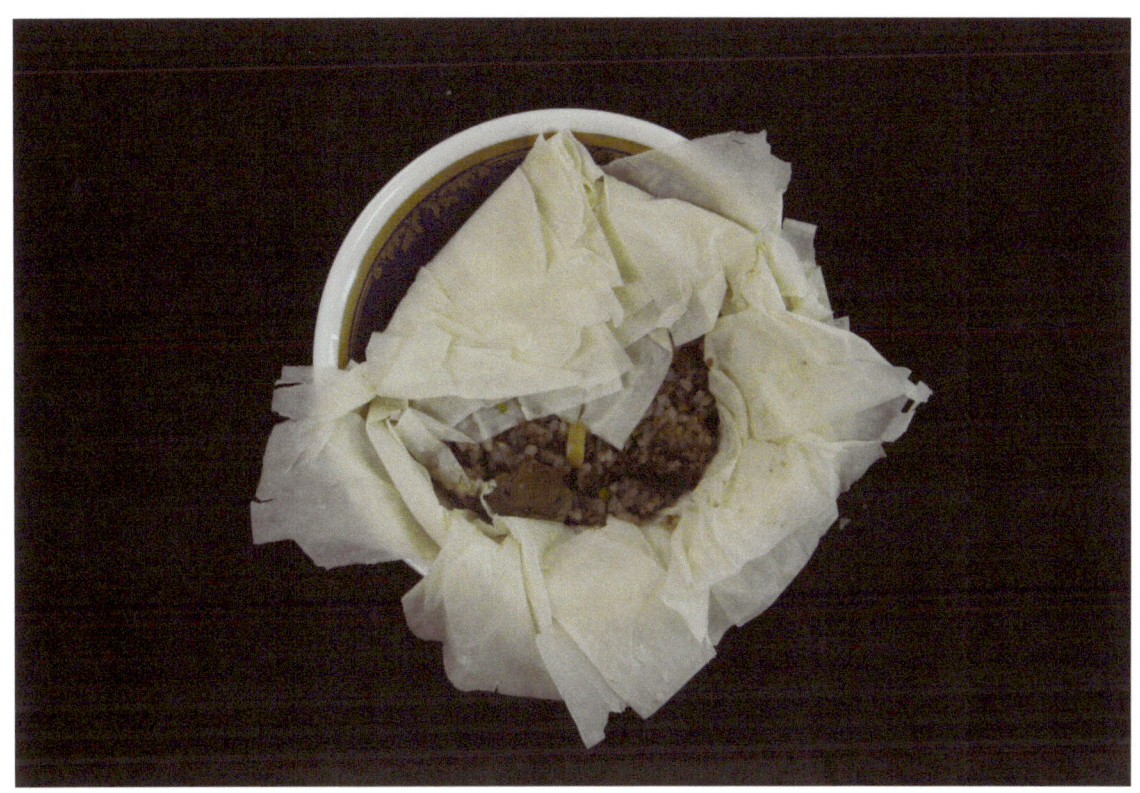

Hajjah Nazihe Adil Kabbani

In Syria, this dish is served on festive occasions.
It is delicious, but time-consuming.

Ingredients
1 lb ground beef
1 large onion
4 teaspoons salt
1 ½ teaspoons pepper
1 ½ teaspoons cinnamon
8 tablespoons butter
½ cup pine nuts (available at Mediterranean markets)

¾ cup blanched almonds (available at Mediterranean markets)
2 ½ cups peas
14 oz can mushrooms (optional)
3 cups short-grain rice
2 packages phyllo dough

Preparation
1. Preheat oven to 500°F.
2. Soak the rice in a bowl with enough hot water to cover by 2 inches.
3. Mince the onion. Brown ground beef and onion in a big pot over medium heat, continuously working the meat with a wooden spoon to achieve a crumbly texture. Once the beef releases and reabsorbs all its juices, add salt, pepper, and cinnamon; mix thoroughly. Remove from heat and set aside to cool.
4. Sauté the pine nuts in 2 tablespoons of the butter over medium heat until golden brown. Add sautéed pine nuts and any pan drippings to the meat mixture; stir.
5. Sauté the almonds in the remaining 2 tablespoons of the butter over medium heat until lightly golden. Add sautéed almonds and any pan drippings to meat mixture. Also stir in peas and mushrooms. If using canned mushrooms, rinse well before adding.
6. Rinse rice in cold water a few times until the water runs clear; drain in a colander.
7. Add five cups of water to the meat. When the water boils, add the rice. Bring to a boil again on high heat. When it boils again, reduce the heat to medium. Cook, covered, over medium heat. When the rice is mostly cooked, and has absorbed most of the water, reduce the heat to low and continue cooking, covered, until the rice is cooked. Remove from heat.
8. Spread out the meat mixture and let cool.
9. Take out small bowls. Take out the pieces of phyllo dough. Fold them in half lengthwise. Put 3 pieces of the folded phyllo dough on top of each other in the small bowl; creating a "bowl" of phyllo dough. Keep the phyllo dough covered and work as quickly as possible to avoid drying out.
10. To assemble the ouzi; place 5 heaping tablespoons of the filling, about ¾ cup of the filling, inside the phyllo-bowl; smooth slightly with the bottom of the spoon to flatten. Then fold the phyllo dough over, starting at one side, and then folding little-by-little. Once filled and covered with the dough, keep your hand on top of the bowl. Turn the bowl over, and

then slide into the baking dish. The smooth side of the phyllo dough should be showing. Every 16-oz box of phyllo dough makes 12 ouzi.

11. Repeat until baking dish is full; spoon ½ tablespoon of melted butter on top of each ouzi.

12. Bake the ouzi in the preheated oven for 8-10 minutes, until lightly golden on top; serve hot.

Serves 12

Chicken and Fish Chapter

Advice on Eating with Children

Hajjah Naziha says, "It is important to always make *du'a* at the table before and after eating, to thank Allah for the food He sent, to thank Him for the blessing of being together with family. You must also ask that Allah put love in our hearts for the Prophet ﷺ, to love and respect all human beings. Allah likes us all to be respectful of one another. It is remembrance that will foster love in our hearts. Thus, we must remember Allah ﷻ and the Prophet ﷺ in our daily life."

Chicken and Potatoes
Patetesli Tavuk Kebab
Cyprus

Ingredients
2 whole chickens cut into pieces
2 tablespoons + ½ teaspoon salt
1 tablespoon + ½ teaspoon pepper
2 tablespoons + ½ teaspoon cinnamon
1 medium onion
12 medium potatoes
4 tablespoons tomato paste
¼ cup olive oil

Preparation
1. Preheat oven to 400F.
2. Season the chicken pieces with ½ teaspoon each of salt, pepper, and cinnamon in a baking pan.
3. Finely chop the onion. Peel potatoes and cut in half. Make a slice in the middle of the potato halves and wiggle knife back and forth to create a slit; being careful not to cut through the potato.
4. In a bowl, mix the remaining salt, pepper, and cinnamon with the potatoes, onions, tomato paste, and olive oil.
5. Add the chicken and potato mixture to the baking pan; mix well.
6. Cover with foil and bake in a preheated oven for 2 hours.
7. Brown the top if desired; serve hot.

Serves 6-8

Fried Chicken
Fripoule
Lebanon

Ingredients
3 eggs
½ cup flour
2 teaspoons salt
1 teaspoon cumin
1 teaspoon paprika
1 teaspoon coriander
1 teaspoon pepper
1 teaspoon cinnamon
1 teaspoon sumac
1 tablespoon cornstarch
½ teaspoon baking powder
2 teaspoons Indian tandoori spice (optional)

2 chickens cut into pieces
Oil for frying

<u>Preparation</u>
1. Mix the eggs, flour, salt, cumin, paprika, coriander, pepper, cinnamon, sumac, cornstarch, baking powder, and tandoori spice.
2. Pour the mixture over the chicken; coat the chicken well. Allow to marinate for at least ½ hour or overnight in the refrigerator.
3. Heat the oil on high heat for frying. When the oil is hot, add the chicken and deep fry until brown. Fry 6-8 pieces of chicken at a time. Fry for 15-20 minutes; turning to cook evenly. Remove the chicken with a slotted spoon and place on a plate lined with paper towel.
4. Serve hot.
Serves 6-8

Fried chicken goes especially well served with french-fried potatoes and green salad.

Indonesian Chicken
Indonesia

Ingredients
2 chickens cut into pieces, skinless
corn oil (for frying)
6 tablespoons crushed garlic
6 tablespoons grated fresh ginger
6 tablespoons coriander powder
6 small chicken bullion cubes
2 cans coconut milk
4 cups water

4 tablespoons tomato paste

Preparation
1. Preheat oven to 400F.
2. Heat the oil on high heat for frying. When the oil is hot, add the chicken and deep fry until golden brown. Fry 6-8 pieces of chicken at a time. Fry for 7-10 minutes on each side; turning to cook evenly. Remove the chicken with a slotted spoon and set aside. Repeat until all the chicken is fried.
3. To prepare the sauce for the chicken sauté the garlic and ginger in ½ cup of the oil used for frying the chicken until it becomes a dark golden color. Add coriander and sauté. Add the chicken bullion, coconut milk, tomato paste, and 4 cups of water.
4. Place the chicken in a baking dish. Pour the sauce over the chicken. Cover and bake in the preheated oven for 1 hour.
5. Serve hot.

Serves 4-6

Hajjah Nazihe Adil Kabbani

Rosemary Chicken with Garlic

Ingredients
6 boneless chicken breasts
1 clove garlic
4 tablespoons olive oil
1 tablespoon fresh rosemary
½ teaspoon salt
½ teaspoon ground black pepper
6 ripe medium tomatoes
sprigs of parsley and lettuce leaves for garnish

Preparation
1. Cut chicken into 2-inch chunks and crush garlic. Sauté garlic in 2 tablespoons olive oil over medium heat for 3 minutes.
2. Heat the remaining 2 tablespoons of oil over medium heat in a Dutch oven or heavy pot. Add chicken pieces, rosemary, salt, and pepper. Sauté for 5 minutes, stirring constantly until chicken is browned.
3. Cut tomatoes into quarters and add to pot along with crushed garlic.
4. Cover and simmer for 30 minutes over medium-low heat or until chicken is tender.
5. Serve hot or cold over a fresh bed of lettuce and garnish with sprigs of parsley.

Serves 6

Salmon with Mashed Potatoes

Ingredients
1 red bell pepper
2 lbs potatoes
½ cup milk
¾ cup half and half
1 ½ teaspoons thyme
1 ½ teaspoons rosemary
1 ½ teaspoons mint
1 ½ teaspoons parsley
1 ½ teaspoons oregano
1 ½ lbs small salmon steaks
4 tablespoons butter

3 tablespoons white vinegar

<u>Preparation</u>
1. Set oven temperature to broil.
2. Place pepper on cookie sheet on top most oven rack. Broil the pepper until skin is charred. Place in a plastic bag and allow to cool. Peel the skin and cut into small pieces.
3. Boil potatoes with salt water until done. Drain and peel. Mash with milk and cream.
4. Chop herbs and sprinkle onto the salmon steaks along with salt and pepper. Set aside for 15 minutes.
5. Melt butter in a deep frying pan over medium heat.
6. Fry salmon steaks skin side up (if there is skin) for 3 minutes. Add vinegar and resume cooking for another 4 minutes or until slightly browned. Flip the salmon over and fry the other side until the fish changes color; the skin side should be dark brown and the skin should come off easily, about 5 minutes.
7. Remove salmon from heat; if desired remove skin.
8. Reheat pepper and potatoes.
9. Place salmon on top of potatoes, garnish with the red pepper and fresh herbs; drizzle with pan juices. Serve hot.

Serves 4

Meat Chapter

Hajjah Amina's *Baraka*

Every Jumu'ah a man would bring Hajjah Amina the shoulder from a baby lamb to use as meat. She would use it to cook until the following Friday. The shoulder has a very small amount of meat. From her *baraka,* that shoulder provided ground meat and bones to cook with throughout the week. Hajjah Amina would cook using just a normal-sized pot for her family and her numerous guests.

She gave a holy chore to her eldest daughter and son, Hajjah Nazihe and Hajj Mehmet. There are poor people in Damascus; not homeless, but they are old and have no family. They have no way of working or preparing food. Every night before dinner, Hajj Mehmet and Hajjah Naziha would go and feed people before they would eat. Hajj Mehmet would take food for 5-6 old men, and Hajjah Naziha would take food for 5-6 old women. These people all lived in different houses; some people lived in the mountains and some close to the mosque. Hajjah Naziha and her brother would spend an hour each day delivering the food before they themselves ate. And they were happy.

Leg of Lamb
Fakhd Kharouf

Lebanon

Ingredients
1 leg of lamb (with bone)
10 garlic cloves
1/8 cup olive oil
2 teaspoons salt
1 teaspoon pepper
2 teaspoons cinnamon

Preparation
1. Preheat oven to 400F.
2. Trim any extra fat from the leg and rinse.
3. Using a knife, make 10 deep incisions in different places on the meat. Insert the whole garlic cloves into these incisions.
4. Combine olive oil, salt, pepper, and cinnamon in a bowl; rub over the entire leg and transfer to a covered baking dish.
5. Bake in preheated oven for 1 hour; remove the leg of lamb from the oven. Make several deep slits into the leg down to the bone; flip the leg over so that the side with the slits is on the bottom. Then repeat on the other side; cut deep slits down to the bone on the top of the leg. This process allows the leg to cook evenly; even where the meat is very thick.
6. Place back in baking dish and return to the oven. Cover and bake for 2 more hours.
7. Transfer to a shallow platter; serve hot.

Serves 6-8

Leg of Lamb with Spring Vegetables

Ingredients
Stock:
2 small shank bones of lamb
1 onion
1 stick celery
1 carrot
6 pepper corns
1 teaspoon salt

Leg of Lamb:
4-5 lb leg of lamb (with bone)
1/4 cup butter
3 cloves garlic
1 tablespoon parsley
1/2 cup vinegar
10 small new potatoes
20 baby carrots
1 cup fresh mushrooms
1 teaspoon sugar
1 tablespoon flour
6 tablespoons light cream
½ teaspoon black pepper
1 teaspoon salt

Preparation
Stock:
Quarter the onion. Quarter the celery and carrot sticks. Place shank bones of lamb in a pot along with the onion, celery, carrot, peppercorns, salt, and enough water to cover.   Bring to

a boil on high heat. Reduce heat to medium low; and simmer, partially uncovered. Remove any foam that may form and simmer for 2 hours or until stock is very concentrated; strain.

Leg of Lamb:
1. Preheat oven at 450°F.
2. Trim skin and fat from leg of lamb. Crush garlic and chop parsley. Cream the butter and add garlic and parsley. Spread over the lamb and set aside for 15 minutes.
3. Place lamb in a large Pyrex (13x9x2) and bake uncovered for 20 minutes.
Note: Shake casserole occasionally to prevent lamb from sticking.
4. Reduce oven temperature to 350°F.
5. Add vinegar to casserole and simmer gently for 15 minutes or until reduced by 1/3.
6. Add 2 cups of stock from shank bone and season with salt and pepper. Cover and bake for 2 hours. Turn the lamb every 30 minutes to prevent it from drying out.
7. Peel potatoes and add to casserole along with carrots; bake for 30 minutes. Add mushrooms and bake for an additional 30 minutes.
8. Strain and reserve gravy from casserole. Turn oven to low add sugar, cover, and keep hot in the oven.
9. For sauce, skim fat from cooking liquid; mix in the flour.
10. Heat in a saucepan stirring until it comes to a boil. Simmer for 2-3 minutes. Add cream and seasoning to taste, simmer for a few more minutes.
11. Arrange meat on a platter and spoon over a little sauce. Surround by vegetables. Serve sauce on the side in a gravy boat. Serve hot.

Serves 6-8

Grandshaykh's Dish: Tender Peppered Beef Smothered in Succulent Onions
Kul Basti
Daghestan

This is called Grandshaykh's Dish. It was one of Grandshaykh Abdullah Daghestani's (q) favorite recipes, and he said that they cooked it in his country. There really are ten onions in this dish! There is no added water, but quite a lot of sauce is produced from the meat and onions.

Ingredients
2½ lbs boneless beef known as "*biftek*" (from Middle Eastern butcher) or "sandwich steak" (from butcher) with no fat

Hajjah Nazihe Adil Kabbani

10 medium onions
2 tablespoons salt
1 tablespoon pepper
¼ cup olive oil

Preparation
1. Cut meat into thin strips which 2 centimeters wide.
2. Thinly slice all the onions into long strips.
3. Cover meat with onions, salt, and pepper.
4. Marinate for at least half an hour or overnight in the refrigerator.
5. Cook over low heat without stirring until the meat has released its juices, for 30-45 minutes. Then stir the meat.
6. Cook over low heat for one to two hours, or until the meat is tender; stirring occasionally.
7. Once the meat is tender, stir in the olive oil and cook for another ten minutes.
8. Transfer to a deep dish and serve hot.
Serves 4-6

Meat Dumplings
Khinkal
Daghestan

This was a favorite dish of Grandshaykh Abdullah al-Faiz ad-Daghestani.

Ingredients
Dough:
(Use Tortellini Soup, Peel Meen, recipe for dough from the Soup Chapter)

Meat filling
2 medium onions
1 ½ lbs ground beef
2 teaspoons salt
1 teaspoon black pepper

Broth
12 cups water
Salt to taste
Accompanying Sauces
½ head of garlic
1 cup yogurt
¾ cup vinegar
¼ cup of cooking liquid from dumplings

Preparation
1. Use Peel Meen recipe and knead dough until it is the consistency of an earlobe. Prepare a floured surface and knead dough in a rolling motion, folding in the far side of the dough towards you. Cover the dough with a towel or bowl and let rest for 10 minutes.
2. Remove dough and form into a tubular shape; divide into 5 pieces and cover with a towel. Allow dough to rest for another 5-10 minutes.
3. Finely chop onion and in a bowl combine with ground beef, salt, and pepper. Take one piece of dough (keeping others covered with the kitchen towel), knead slightly, and roll it out. If it does not roll out easily sprinkle flour on top or flip dough over. Roll dough out very thin, 1/16 inch or thinner if possible.
Note: You might have some meat filling left over depending how thin or thick you roll out the dough.

4. Using a biscuit cutter or glass, cut out circles from the dough (about 3.6 inches in diameter); using as much of the dough as possible. Place 1 teaspoon of meat filling in the middle of each circle. Next, on the side farthest from your body pinch dough together to form the beginning of a half moon shape. While holding the meat in with left thumb, pinch one side in then the other as if French braiding and pinch end securely. (Or if this is too difficult, just pinch edges together to close the circle in a half moon shape like for the *Shishbarak*).

5. Repeat until all the dough is finished. Also re-roll any left over scraps. Arrange dumplings in a single layer on a tray, not touching, and cover with a towel.

6. In a large pot bring water and salt to a boil over high heat. Reduce heat to medium. Add dumplings one at a time. Cook 5-7 minutes or until tender. The dumplings should become translucent and float. Do not cook more than 30 dumplings in one batch. If more than 30 dumplings are made, boil 30, transfer to a platter and boil the rest. Reserve ¼ cup of the cooking liquid.

7. To prepare the first sauce, crush 3-7 cloves of garlic (more or less to taste) and mix with yogurt. This can also be done in a blender. The sauce should be a thick consistency.

8. To prepare the second sauce, blend ¾ cup vinegar with 3-4 crushed cloves of garlic (more or less to taste), and about ¼ cup of the dumpling cooking liquid. This sauce should be of a thinner consistency.

9. Serve the dumplings with the yogurt and vinegar sauces in separate bowls on the side.

Serves 8

Ravioli with Yogurt
Shishbarak
Lebanon

Ingredients
Dough:
(Use Tortellini Soup, Peel Meen, recipe for dough from the Soup Chapter)

Stuffing:
2 lbs ground beef
1 large onion
4 tablespoons butter

¼ cup pine nuts
2 teaspoons cinnamon
4 teaspoons salt
2 teaspoons black pepper

Sauce:
12 cups yogurt
3 egg whites
6 cups water
4 tablespoons crushed garlic
2 bunches cilantro, (2 cups)
3 teaspoons salt
2 tablespoons cornstarch

Topping:
½ cup butter and ½ cup pine nuts

Preparation
1. Use Peel Meen recipe to knead dough until it is the consistency of an earlobe. Let stand at least ½ hour.
2. To prepare filling, mince onion. Brown ground beef and onion over medium-low heat, continuously working the meat with a wooden spoon to achieve a crumbly texture. Simmer long enough to allow the beef to absorb all liquid in pan. Add salt, pepper, and cinnamon.
3. In separate pan fry pine nuts in butter until golden. Add to meat mixture along with any pan juices.

4. Roll flour into long tube and cut into 4 equal pieces and cover with a towel to avoid drying out.

To roll out dough, prepare a floured surface. Remove one piece of dough from the covered bowl and roll out to 1/8 inch thickness. Using a water glass cut round pieces out of the rolled-out dough.

Repeat with remaining dough pieces.

5. Inside each small, round piece, place 1 teaspoon of meat mixture.
6. Fold circle in half and press the edges firmly to ensure they do not open. Bring the ends of the dough together and pinch well. Each piece should closely resemble an Italian tortellini.
7. Place each prepared piece side by side in a tray making sure not to place on top of each other. Keep the tray covered with a kitchen towel as you prepare the rest of the Shishbarak.
8. In another large pot over medium-high heat mix yogurt, egg whites, salt, and 6 cups of water; stirring occasionally until it comes to a boil. Reduce heat to low and add each piece of Shishbarak. Cook approximately 10-15 minutes.
9. Mince the cilantro. Add garlic and cilantro.
10. When pasta is cooked combine 2 tablespoons cornstarch and ½ cup water and add to pot. Stir gently into pot and then turn heat off.
11. In a saucepan, melt the
11. Transfer to a deep serving dish; garnish with ½ cup melted butter.
12. Serve with white rice.

Serves 6-8

Eggplant Stuffed with Lamb
Karnı Yarık
Ottoman Empire

Ingredients
8 thin eggplants
sunflower oil or corn oil for frying

Filling:
½ lb ground lamb or beef, or combination
1 small onion
¼ cup fresh parsley or 1 Tablespoons dried
¼ cup fresh mint or 1 Tablespoons dried
¼ cup fresh dill or 1 Tablespoons dried
1 tomato
3-4 cloves garlic
1 tablespoon tomato paste
1 tablespoon pine nuts

1 teaspoon ground cinnamon
1 teaspoon ground allspice
1 tablespoon olive oil
1 teaspoon salt
½ teaspoon fresh ground pepper

Topping:
½ green bell pepper, halved lengthwise and cut into 4 long slices
1 tomato, thinly sliced

Cooking Sauce:
4 tablespoons olive oil
4 tablespoons water
juice of ½ lemon
1 teaspoon sugar

Preparation
1. Peel each eggplant into zebra stripes and soak in salted water for 1 hour.
2. Preheat oven to 400°F.
3. Finely chop onion and herbs; blanch and finely chop tomato. Crush garlic. Mix with 1 teaspoon of salt. In a large bowl, using your hands, mix together all ingredients for the filling. Knead well for 10 minutes, until ingredients resemble a paste.
4. Drain eggplant and dry with towel.
5. Heat enough oil in a pan to fry each eggplant whole.
6. Fry each eggplant over medium-low heat until golden brown. Transfer to a shallow baking dish.
7. Cut each eggplant open lengthwise, from end to end. Do not cut through bottom of eggplant. Gently pry them open with tines of a fork. Stuff until all filling is used and eggplants look like canoes.
8. Garnish tops with one slice of bell pepper and tomato.

9. Mix all ingredients for cooking sauce and spoon over each eggplant. Cover baking dish with foil. Bake 25-30 minutes; remove foil and bake additional 40 minutes or until meat is tender and all liquid has evaporated.
10. Serve hot or cold.

Serves 4

Stuffed Mushrooms with Ground Beef

Ingredients
½ lb ground beef
1 medium onion
2 teaspoons salt
1 teaspoon pepper
1 teaspoon cinnamon
¼ cup pine nuts
20 medium white mushrooms
3 Tablespoons corn oil or butter
1/8 cup lemon juice
1 cup water

Preparation
1. Preheat the oven to 400F.
2. Finely chop the onion and mince the parsley. Sauté the ground beef and onion together over medium-low heat, stirring occasionally until the meat releases and reabsorbs its own juices. Mix in a teaspoon each of the salt, pepper, cinnamon.
3. In another pan, sauté the pine nuts in the corn oil or butter until golden brown. Add the pine nuts and their oil to the meat,
4. Spoon a table spoonful of the ground beef into each mushroom.
5. Place in a large Pyrex baking dish. Mix the water, lemon juice, and the remaining teaspoon of the salt.
6. Bake for 20 minutes at 400F.

Serve hot or warm.
Serves 6-8

Stuffed Tomatoes with Green Bell Peppers
Etli Domateslı Dolması

Turkey

Ingredients

2 lbs firm red tomatoes
½ lb sweet, round, green bell pepper
1 lb ground beef
2 medium onions, finely diced
3 tablespoons butter
¼ cup pine nuts
4 cloves garlic
1 ½ teaspoons salt
½ teaspoon black pepper
½ teaspoon cinnamon
¼ cup lemon juice
1 teaspoon dried mint

Preparation
1. Preheat oven to 400°F.
2. Wash all vegetables well and set aside to dry.
3. Finely chop onion and fry with ground beef in 1 tablespoon of butter over medium heat. Add 1 teaspoon salt, pepper and cinnamon and stir.
Remove pan from heat and set aside.
5. In a separate pan, roast pine nuts in 1 tablespoon of butter over medium heat. Until golden brown. Remove from heat and mix pine nuts and pan drippings into the ground beef.
6. Cut a round piece from the top of each tomato and reserve.
Remove tomato pulp with a spoon, leaving some flesh inside to help the tomato hold its shape while cooking; reserve pulp. Stuff tomatoes with the meat mixture and close with the round piece cut from the top.
7. Cut a round piece from the top of each bell pepper and reserve.
Remove the seeds and the white part from the inside.

Stuff peppers with the meat mixture and close with the round piece cut from the top.

8. Transfer tomatoes and peppers to a casserole dish or baking pan.

9. Crush the garlic and mix with remaining ½ teaspoon salt and the reserved tomato pulp. Add lemon juice, mint, and 1 tablespoon butter.

Pour this mixture over the stuffed tomatoes and green peppers.

10. Cover the dish with foil and bake in the preheated oven for 50 minutes, or until vegetables are tender.

11. Serve hot with rice.

Serves 4-6

Stuffed Zucchini and Eggplant
Cousa Batenjan Mahshi
Middle East

Ingredients
Filling:
2 lbs baby eggplant*
2 lbs baby zucchini*
1 cup uncooked rice
1 lbs uncooked ground beef
½ teaspoon salt
¼ teaspoon ground black pepper
¼ teaspoon cinnamon

*Vegetables should be uniform in size, about 6 inches long.

Sauce:
5 tablespoons tomato paste
5 cups water
2 teaspoons salt
1/4 cup lemon juice
5 cloves garlic
2 tablespoons dried mint

Preparation
1. Preheat oven to 350°F.
2. Wash and dry vegetables. Cut the tops off of the vegetables. Using a large carving tool, hollow-out vegetables, starting from the top, making a ½ inch hole down the center of the vegetable. (Do not hollow through other end of vegetable)
3. Rinse rice in cold water a few times until the water runs clear. Mix uncooked rice with meat and season with salt, pepper, and cinnamon.
4. Stuff the vegetables firmly with the rice-meat mixture and place in a 13x9x2 Pyrex dish.

5. Crush garlic and in a bowl combine with tomato paste, water, salt, lemon juice, and mint. Pour gently over the stuffed vegetables.
6. Cover and bake for 1 hour or until stuffing is thoroughly cooked and vegetables are tender. Serve hot.

Serves 8

Hajjah Nazihe Adil Kabbani

Meatloaf with Eggs and Peas
Kafta ma'al Bazalla wal-Bayd
Lebanon

Ingredients
1 medium onion
½ bunch parsley (½ cup)
6 eggs
1 lb ground beef
2 teaspoons salt
1½ teaspoons pepper
1 teaspoon cinnamon
2 cups frozen peas

Preparation
1. Finely chop the onion and parsley; hard-boil 5 of the eggs.
2. Using your hands knead together the ground beef, onion, parsley, salt, pepper, and cinnamon.
4. Preheat oven to 350 F.

Method 1 for filling the meat with the eggs and peas:

Layer plastic wrap over a cutting board. Flatten the meat mixture on the board. Place the whole eggs and defrosted peas in the middle of the meat mixture. Pick up one side of the plastic wrap and bring it up to the middle. Pick on the other side of the plastic wrap and bring it to the middle. Press the meat together in the middle and on the ends to cover the peas and eggs. Lightly oil the baking dish. Carefully lift the plastic wrap up with the log shaped meat on it, place at the edge of the baking dish, and let it roll off the plastic wrap. Make sure to do this transfer carefully so the meat does not fall apart. The sealed end of the meat should be facing up.

Method 2 for filling the meat with the eggs and peas:
Spread the entire meat mixture on the bottom of a 15 inch long baking pan. Place the eggs down the middle of the mixture. Add the peas on top of the eggs. Carefully fold one side of the meat up to meet the eggs and peas. Then fold the other side up in the same manner. Seal the top and ends of the mound-shaped meat with your fingers.
5. Bake uncovered at 350 F for two hours. Serve hot.

Serves 4-6

Kafta with Potatoes
Lebanon

Ingredients
Kefta:
2 onions
1 tablespoon Italian parsley
2 lbs ground beef
1 tablespoon salt
1/2 tablespoon pepper
1/2 tablespoon cinnamon
1/2 tablespoon cumin powder
1/2 cup pine nuts
3-4 tablespoons tomato paste
1/3 cup lemon juice
2 tablespoons salt

Potatoes: (see Home Style French Fries *Battata Maqlia* from the Vegetable Sides Chapter)

Preparation
1. Preheat oven to 300°F.
2. Chop onions and parsley; mix thoroughly with ground beef, salt, pepper, cinnamon, and cumin. Using your hands, make small flat patties with the meat mixture, about the size of your palm. Place 4-5 pine nuts in the middle of the patty fold over the edges of the meat to cover pine nuts and flatten a bit with you hands.
3. Place patties in an un-greased baking pan and bake for 30 minutes. Turn the patties over and cook the other side for 20 minutes. Set aside.
4. To make the sauce, in a large bowl mix the tomato paste, lemon juice, salt, and about two cups of water.
5. Place the french-fried potatoes on top of the patties and add the sauce to barely cover the meat and potatoes.

6. Return to oven and bake uncovered at 300°F until the sauce comes to a boil and the water evaporates a bit.
7. Serve with salad and pita bread. Serve hot.

Serves 6-8

Savory Ground Beef with Tomato Wedges
Kafta bi-Siniyya
Syria

Ingredients
½ bunch parsley (½ cup)
1 large onion
2 lbs ground beef
1 Tablespoon salt
1 teaspoon pepper
2 teaspoons cinnamon
1 teaspoon cumin
6 large tomatoes

Preparation
1. Preheat oven to 300F.
2. Mince the parsley and finely chop the onion. Using your hands, knead together the ground beef, onion, parsley, salt, pepper, cinnamon, and cumin in a large bowl.
Note: For even better taste, this mixture can be made the day before and refrigerated overnight.
3. Spread the meat mixture evenly across the bottom of a large baking dish; pat down firmly.
4. Slice the tomatoes approximately ½-inch thick and arrange in a decorative pattern over the meat.
5. Bake uncovered at 300F until the juices partially evaporate.
Reduce heat to 200F and continue to cook uncovered for an additional 20-30 minutes.
Note: Do not bake until all of the liquid has evaporated as this will dry out the meat.
6. Slice as you would a pizza and serve hot.
Serve with French fries, salad, and pita bread.
Serves 4-6

Hajjah Nazihe Adil Kabbani

Ground Beef and Spaghetti Casserole
Fırında Macarna
Cyprus

This is the first dish Hajjah Naziha ever made in a home economics summer class she attended when she was 13. Her teachers name was Saliha.

Ingredients
2 tablespoons olive oil
3½ teaspoons salt
2 packages spaghetti
1 medium onion
1 lb ground beef
1 bunch parsley (1 cup)
1 teaspoon pepper
1 teaspoon cinnamon
3 cups mozzarella or white cheddar cheese
½ cup butter + 2 tablespoons butter
½ cup flour
4½ cups whole milk
5 eggs

Preparation
1. Preheat oven to 350F.
2. Bring a large pot of water to a boil; add the olive oil and ½ teaspoon of the salt. Add spaghetti to the pot, without breaking. Prepare the spaghetti according to the directions on the package. Strain spaghetti and rinse with cold water, to avoid overcooking.
3. Finely chop the onion and mince the parsley. Sauté the ground beef and onion together over medium-low heat, stirring occasionally until the meat releases and reabsorbs its own juices. Mix in a teaspoon each of the salt, pepper, cinnamon, and half of the parsley.
4. Grate cheese and combine with remaining half of the parsley.
5. Using 1 tablespoon of the butter, grease a large rectangular Pyrex baking dish (15 inches x 10 inches x 2 inches) or a large round metal pan (18 inches in diameter and 2½-inches deep available at Middle Eastern markets) with 2 tablespoons of the butter. Spread approximately 1/3 of the spaghetti evenly in a layer on the bottom of the pan.
6. Next, spread all the ground beef in an even layer on top of the spaghetti; pat flat with

your hand.

7. Layer another third of the spaghetti evenly in a layer on top of the ground beef. Spread the cheese and parsley mixture in an even layer on top of the spaghetti.

8. Layer the last third of the spaghetti evenly in a layer on top of the cheese.

Béchamel Sauce:

1. in a large sauce pan, melt ½ cup of butter. Whisk the melted butter with the flour over medium heat until evenly blended and an even golden color.

2. Whisk in the whole milk, eggs, and the remaining salt. Continue stirring with a whisk until the mixture thickens and becomes the consistency of pudding.

 Note: Eggs add flavor to an otherwise plain Béchamel Sauce sauce.

3. Pour the Béchamel Sauce sauce over the casserole, starting in the middle and moving the ingredients so that the sauce covers the entire top layer of noodles. The sauce is thick enough that it should "sit" on top of the other ingredients and not sink to the bottom.

4. Bake uncovered on the middle rack of the preheated oven for 30 minutes, or until golden brown. Serve hot.

Serves 6-8

Meat and Potato Pie
Belish
Russia

When Hajjah Nazihe was young, she and her family would visit her grandmother every Friday. Friday is the Muslim holiday, a day of prayer and an occasion to visit family and friends. Hajjah Nazihe's grandmother would prepare this dish as symbol of celebration and joy when all the kids came to visit. Everyone loves it!

Ingredients
2½ lbs beef or lamb
6 medium potatoes
2½ cups water

½ cup plain yogurt
1½ tablespoons salt
½ cup butter
1 large onion
7 cups flour
1 tablespoon + 1 teaspoon pepper
1 egg

Preparation
1. Preheat the oven to 350F.
2. Cut the beef into ½ inch cubes. Peel the potatoes and chop into ¾ inch cubes.
3. In a large metal bowl, combine water and yogurt; add salt and stir. Melt 2 tablespoons of the butter and add to the bowl; mix.
4. Mix in the flour with one hand, keeping one hand in the bowl for kneading and one hand out of the bowl to hold the bowl still. Remove the dough from the bowl and knead on the counter until it is the texture and consistency of an earlobe. If the dough is too sticky or thin, add more flour. If it is too dry, dampen your hands and work into the dough mixture. Cover the dough with the overturned bowl and set aside.
5. In another bowl, combine the meat, potatoes, and season with the salt and pepper.
6. Using 1 tablespoon of the butter, grease a large rectangular Pyrex baking dish (15 inches x 10 inches x 2 inches) or a large round metal pan (18 inches in diameter and 2½-inches deep available at Middle Eastern markets).
7. Take one third of the dough and roll it into a ball; reserve under the overturned bowl. Take the remaining 2/3 of the dough and roll it out for the bottom of the pan. Roll out the dough into a ¼-inch thickness in the shape of a large rectangle or circle, depending on dish size. The dough should be a few inches larger than the baking pan because the bottom dough should come up the sides of the pan.
Note: Sprinkle water on the rolling pin to avoid sticking to the dough.
8. Lay the rolled-out dough on the bottom of the pan. Then place the meat mixture on top of the dough. Dot the top of the meat mixture with 5 tablespoons of butter.
9. Roll out the remaining 1/3 of dough a little bit smaller than the size of baking dish used. Place rolled out dough on top of the meat mixture. Bring the edges of the bottom and top

pieces of dough together. Press the bottom and top piece of dough together to seal, like as you would for a pie crust.

Make a hole in the center of the top piece of dough. Take a piece of leftover dough and form it into a ball about 1 inch in diameter; place on top of the hole.

Note: There are no slits or cuts in this dough. It should be completely sealed so that the steam will thoroughly cook the filling.

10. Beat an egg in a bowl and brush over the top. This will give the pie a nice shine when baked.

11. Bake in the middle rack of a 350F for 2½ hours. The top should be a golden color. To ensure that the pie is completely done before serving gently remove the ball of dough from the top, and withdraw a piece of potato with a fork. If the potato is cooked; the Belish is ready to serve. If the potato is not cooked, cover with foil and return to the oven for an additional 15 minutes. Test again before serving.

12. The crust, when served, will be a little tough as this is not a soft crust. Serve hot.

Serves 6-8

Braise Chapter

The meat dishes in this section are called "*yekhni*" in Arabic which consists of a meat and vegetable cooked together. Here we refer to them as braises since they are served as a saucy companion to rice. Meat braises are a practical main dish since the ingredients are simmered together in one pot, making cleanup more convenient. Traditionally braises are placed on the table in a deep serving bowl alongside rice.

Spinach and Meatball Braise
Cyprus

Ingredients
Meatballs:
1 medium onion
½ bunch parsley (½ cup)
2 teaspoons salt
1 teaspoon pepper
1 teaspoon cinnamon
1 lb ground beef
½ cup corn oil

Braise:
3½ lbs fresh spinach
3 tablespoons tomato paste
¾ cup lemon juice
7 cups water
5 teaspoons salt
¼ teaspoon pepper
2 teaspoons cinnamon

Preparation
Meatballs:
1. Finely chop onion; wash and mince parsley.
2. Using your hands, knead together the onion, parsley, salt, pepper, and cinnamon. Once well combined, knead in the ground beef; let stand for 10
minutes.
3. Roll the meat into meatballs ¾-inch in diameter, using about a teaspoonful of meat per meatball.
4. Warm the oil in a soup pot over high heat. Add the meatballs and sauté until dark brown; turning occasionally to cook evenly. Remove meatballs and set aside.

Braise Preparation

1. Wash and chop the spinach and stems; bring to a boil in water over high heat. Boil the spinach for five minutes until wilted and a darker green in color. Drain and rinse with cold water. Squeeze any water out of the spinach and set aside.
2. In a small bowl, mix the tomato paste and lemon juice; stir into the meatballs. Add the spinach and 7 cups of water to the pot. Mix in the salt, pepper, and cinnamon. Bring to a boil over high heat.
3. Reduce the heat to medium and simmer for 15 minutes if using a pressure cooker. If using a regular pot, increase simmer time to 30 minutes.
4. Transfer to a deep serving bowl. Serve hot.

Serves 4-6

Flat Green Bean and Beef Chunk Braise
Lubya bil-Lahma
Lebanon

Ingredients
3 lbs beef chunks
¼ cup corn oil
4 teaspoons salt
oil (for frying)
4 lbs flat green beans (available in Mediterranean markets; they are wide and flat, and called "*lubiyya*" or "*fusiliya khudra areeda*" in Arabic)
1 tablespoon pepper
3 tablespoons cinnamon

Preparation

1. Warm the oil in a pressure cooker or regular pot over medium-high heat. When the oil is hot, sauté the meat until evenly brown.
2. Meanwhile heat the oil for the beans in a separate pot over high heat. Add a teaspoon of the salt to the oil to avoid splattering. Once the oil is hot, deep-fry the beans until lightly golden; turning occasionally to cook evenly. When all the beans are fried, mix the beans into the meat in the pressure cooker. Add nine cups of water to cover the beans.
Also, add the remaining salt, pepper, and cinnamon.
3. Cover and bring to a boil over high heat. Reduce the heat to medium and simmer for 20 minutes. If using a regular pot, increase cooking time to 40 minutes or until beef chunks are tender.
4. Transfer to a deep serving bowl. Serve hot.

Serves 6-8

Green Beans and Meat Chunk Braise
Etli Yeşil Fasulye
Cyprus

Ingredients
4½ lbs green beans, fresh or frozen
2 medium onions
2 large tomatoes
2½ lbs boneless beef chunks
¼ cup corn oil
5 cups water
2 tablespoons plus 1 teaspoon salt
1 tablespoon pepper
¼ cup lemon juice

Preparation
1. If using frozen green beans, rinse and squeeze out any excess water from the beans. Cut the ends off green beans and slice down the middle lengthwise, then cut into 1½ inch pieces across. Finely chop the onions and grate the tomatoes.
2. Cut the meat into 1-inch chunks.
3. Warm a pressure cooker or regular pot over medium heat without any oil; add the meat chunks and brown. Cook until the meat has released and reabsorbed its own juices.
4. Add ¼ cup of corn oil to the meat in the pot; increase the heat to high. When the oil is hot, add the beans and sauté with the meat for ten minutes or until the beans are darker green in color. Stir constantly to prevent the mixture from sticking.
5. Add 5 cups of water along with salt, pepper, and lemon juice. If using a pressure cooker, cover and bring to a boil over high heat. Reduce the heat to medium and cook for 30 minutes. If using a regular pot, increase cooking time to 60 minutes or until the beef chunks are tender.
6. Transfer to a deep serving bowl. Serve hot.
Serves 4-6

Molokhiya with Beef Chunk Braise
Etli Molokhiya
Cyprus

The King's Dish

Molokhiya leaves derive their name from the word "*Malek*," or "*Maleka*," which was used to denote "King" during the Umayyid Caliphate. Only the amirs (princes) and caliphs ate these leaves, ordinary people were not permitted to enjoy this dish. When the Umayyad dynasty fell and the Abbasids came into power they changed the name of this leaf from "*Maleka*" to "*Molokhiya*" and the average person was allowed to savor it as well.

Ingredients
2 lbs meat chunks (better with bones)
1 large onion
4-5 medium tomatoes
2 tablespoons tomato paste
½ cup lemon juice
12 cups water
1 lb dry Molokhiya leaves (about 14 handfuls)
Note: Molokhiya leaves are available at Mediterranean or Arab store.
¾ cup corn oil
3 teaspoons salt
3 teaspoons pepper
1 head of garlic
½ cup olive oil

Note: Use one very full handful of Molokhiya leaves per person.

Preparation
1. Soak the leaves in hot water for half an hour.
2. Wash the meat and cut into 2 inch cubes. Heat the pressure cooker or pot on high heat. Add the meat and sauté, without adding any oil until the meat releases and reabsorbs its own juices. Add the salt and pepper.
3. Finely chop and sauté the onion with the meat until the onion is soft and tender. Peel the tomatoes, and chop into large cubes. Add 4-5 fresh tomatoes and sauté until soft. Add tomato paste, ¼ cup of the lemon juice, and water.
4. Drain the Molokhiya leaves in a fine mesh strainer and rinse with cold water. Pick up the leaves, a fistful at a time, and tightly squeeze to release the slippery substance from the leaves. Add the washed Molokhiya leaves to the meat mixture and stir. Break the garlic head into cloves. Stir the garlic cloves into the meat and Molokhiya
5. If using a pressure cooker, cover and bring to a boil over high heat. Reduce the heat to medium and cook for 40 minutes. If using a regular pot, increase cooking time to an hour and a half.

6. When the leaves are softened and the meat is cooked, add ½ cup olive oil and the remaining lemon juice. Simmer for 10 more minutes to thicken.
Note: The Molokhiya leaves must be soft. Too much lemon juice will make them hard, so half of the lemon juice is added after cooking.
7. Transfer to a deep serving bowl and serve hot.

Serves 6-8
Serve with white rice and fresh white pearl onions.

Eggplant with Meat Chunk Braise
Yekhnit Batinjan bil-Lahma
Middle East

This is one of Sajeda Kabbani's favorite dishes.

Ingredients
2 lbs beef chunks
1 onion
1 tablespoon + 1 teaspoon salt
2 teaspoons pepper
1 teaspoon cinnamon
6 lbs eggplants

salt for sprinkling on the eggplant
4 tablespoons tomato paste
4¼ cups water
½ cup corn oil
2 heads garlic
½ cup lemon juice

Preparation

1. Cut the beef into pieces the size of a "bird's head," an inch long and 1/8 inch thick.
2. Heat a large pot over high heat. When hot, without any oil, brown the meat over medium heat. Sauté the meat until it releases and reabsorbs its own juices. Finely chop the onion. Add the chopped onion, salt, pepper, and cinnamon to the meat.
3. Peel eggplants and cut into ¾ inch cubes; sprinkle with salt to remove bitter juices.
4. Dissolve 4 tablespoons of tomato paste in ¼ cup water. Stir the tomato paste and lemon juice into the meat along with corn oil and simmer for a couple of minutes. Then add 4 cups of water.
5. Squeeze the eggplant cubes to remove any bitter juices; add to the meat mixture along with whole garlic cloves and the remaining ¼ cup of lemon juice. Bring to a boil over high heat. Cover the pot and reduce the heat to medium.
6. Simmer, covered, for 45 minutes-1 hour, or until the meat is tender.
7. Transfer to a dish and serve hot.

Serves 6-8

Dessert Chapter

Hajjah Naziha's Young Mind

When Hajjah Naziha was ten years old she would help her parents by guiding the visiting murids around the city of Damascus. She wouldn't lose any of the murids. She would go to the front of the group and say, "Don't run." Then she would go to the back and say, "Go slow" and that way she wouldn't lose any people.

She would tell the bus driver who was taking them around, "Don't rush, I have a lot of people" so he wouldn't leave without the stragglers.

One woman intending to go on Hajj was elderly and very fat. She couldn't move very well, and they didn't know how to get her on the bus. Hajjah Nazihe figured it out. She told the lady to take a step up and then grab the bar on the bus, and then Hajjah Nazihe lifted her second foot up onto the next step. The lady was very happy and said, "No one knows how to get me on the bus, but this little girl who has a big mind."

Rice Pudding
Muhallabiyyah
Lebanon

Ingredients
1 cup short grain rice
8 cups milk
2 cups sugar
1/2 cup pistachios, finely chopped
1 cup water
2 Tablespoons cornstarch dissolved in 1/4 cup water

Preparation

1. Wash the rice. Put in a pot with water and bring to a boil. When the rice is tender, strain and set aside.
2. In a separate pot, heat the milk on high heat. Once the milk has boiled, add the rice to the milk.
3. Slowly stir the sugar into the milk and rice. Stir constantly to avoid burning the milk.
4. In a small bowl, dissolve the cornstarch in 1/4 cup of cold water. Stir the dissolved cornstarch into the milk and rice.
5. Stir in the orange blossom water.
6. Place in individual bowls and decorate with the pistachios. Let chill in the refrigerator.
7. Serve chilled

Serves 6

Baked Apples and Pears

Ingredients
3 apples (any juicy, sweet variety)
Bartlett pears (or any juicy variety)
1/4 of a stick of salted butter
1 1/2 - 2 teaspoons ground cinnamon
6-8 teaspoons of packed brown sugar
36 raisins (optional)
6 teaspoonfuls of chopped walnuts (optional)
24 whole cloves

Preparation
1. Preheat oven to 350°F.
2. Cut the apples and pears in half. Remove seeds and stems with a paring knife or small spoon. Place the apple and pear halves into a 13x9x2-inch Pyrex baking dish.
3. Cut dime-sized pieces of butter into the center of each fruit half.
4. Sprinkle liberally with cinnamon. Place 2 cloves in each half with 3 raisins or 1/2 teaspoon of walnuts.
5. Pack a heaping 1/2 teaspoon of brown sugar in the center of each fruit half, well over the butter, cloves, raisins, and/or walnuts. Bake for 45 minutes.
6. Serve warm with a scoop of vanilla ice cream. Spoon glaze over the ice cream.

Serves 6

Stuffed Oranges with Orange Sorbet

Ingredients
10 juicy oranges
1-2 cups orange juice
1 tablespoon orange blossom water
2 cups powdered sugar
Mint leaves for garnish

Preparation
1. Cut oranges in half and juice them in an electric juicer.
2. Reserve 12 orange halves. Remove the orange pulp from the reserved orange halves with a spoon; you may have to peel certain parts with your hand. In the end, you should have twelve hollow orange halves with little or no pulp remaining inside.

3. Place the halves in a freezer on a tray or stacked inside each other in a freezer bag. They should chill for at least 4-5 hours or overnight in the freezer.

4. Strain the orange juice to remove any pulp. You should have about 5 cups of fresh orange juice. Add 1 cup of orange juice, or enough to have a total of 6 cups of juice. Mix the juice in a bowl with the orange blossom water. Add 2 cups of powdered sugar; mix well.

(Note: If using an ice cream machine, chill the orange juice mixture and follow manufacturer's directions; skip to Step 9.)

5. Pour into a shallow 15x10x2, Pyrex dish so the mixture is about 1-inch deep all around. Place in the freezer.

6. After 1 1/2 hours, take the dish out of the freezer and mix with a fork until a slushy consistency; return to the freezer.

7. Repeat Step 5.

8. Freeze another 2 1/2 hours or until hard to the touch.

9. Remove frozen orange halves from freezer and fill with sorbet. Add a mint leaf on top of each. Place in Pyrex dish and freeze for another hour.

10. Serve cold.

Coconut Pudding

Ingredients
1 7-oz bag grated coconut
6 cups whole milk
1 14-oz can coconut milk
1 1/2 cups sugar
1 1/4 teaspoons coconut extract
7 tablespoons
 cornstarch
1 1/2 cups cold whipping cream
1/4 cup powdered sugar

Preparation
1. Preheat the oven to 350°F. Toast the coconut on a baking sheet for 7-12 minutes, mixing 4-5 times until golden brown; being careful not to burn the coconut.
2. Whisk the milk, coconut milk, sugar, and coconut extract in a bowl until well-combined. Pour mixture into a heavy-bottomed pot; stir in the cornstarch.
3. Place pot over medium heat; stir constantly until thick and bubbling. Turn off the heat and add half of the toasted coconut.
4. Ladle the pudding into individual pudding dishes. Place in the refrigerator for 3-4 hours.
5. Whip the cream and powdered sugar until stiff; set aside.
6. Put a dollop of whip cream on top of each pudding dish. Garnish with remaining toasted coconut.
7. Serve cold.

Serves 6-8

Apricot Compote

Ingredients
16 cups water juice of 1 medium lemon
2 1/4 cups sugar
1 1/4 tablespoons whole cloves
5 cinnamon sticks
3 cups dried Turkish apricots
1 tablespoon cornstarch
1/2 cup cold water

Preparation
1. Bring the water, lemon juice, sugar, cloves, and cinnamon sticks to a boil over medium-high heat. Boil rapidly for 5 minutes; remove from heat. Remove half of the cloves with a slotted spoon.
2. Add apricots and stirring occasionally simmer over medium-low heat for 35-40 minutes or until the apricots are soft. Remove the cinnamon sticks.
3. In a separate bowl, mix the cornstarch and cold water very well, until there are no lumps.
4. When the apricots are soft, pour in the cornstarch mixture and simmer together for 1 more minute. Remove from heat.
5. Place in refrigerator and chill. Transfer to individual serving dishes.

Serves 6-8

Milk and Orange Layered Upside-Down Pudding

Ingredients
4 cups orange juice
1/2 cup sugar
8 tablespoons cornstarch
4 cups whole milk
1 cup sugar
1 teaspoon vanilla

Heavenly Foods

Preparation
1. Heat the orange juice and sugar in a pot over medium heat. Whisking constantly add 4 tablespoons of the cornstarch until thickened to the consistency of gravy.
2. Pour into 7 pudding bowls; bowls should be filled halfway. Let cool for 5-10 minutes, or until pudding develops a thin "skin" on top. It is important to have the skin on top before you add the milk layer so the two layers do not mix.
3. Heat the milk, 1/2 cup of the sugar, and vanilla in a heavy-bottomed pot. Whisking constantly add the remaining 4 tablespoons of cornstarch until thickened to the consistency of gravy.
4. Ladle the milk and sugar carefully and slowly on top of orange pudding to fill the pudding bowls. See picture. Chill 4-5 hours, or overnight.
5. Immediately prior to serving, put a serving plate on top of the bowl and turn upside-down. Remove the bowl. The orange pudding should be on top. Repeat with all the bowls.
6. Serve chilled.

Serves 7

Chocolate Dream Cake

Ingredients
2 eggs, separated
1 teaspoon vanilla
2 ¼ cups flour
1 2/3 cups sugar
1/3 cup cocoa powder
1 ¼ teaspoon baking soda
1 teaspoon baking powder
1 ¼ cup water
¾ cup Crisco or vegetable oil

Filling:
2 cups fresh raspberries or chopped strawberries mixed with 1 tablespoon sugar and slightly mashed with fork.

Topping:
4 cups prepared whipped cream
10 maraschino cherries

Preparation
1. Preheat oven to 375°F.
2. In a bowl beat egg whites and vanilla until stiff peaks form.
3. Sift dry ingredients into a bowl.
4. Add, water, oil and egg yolks. Beat for 1 minute on slow speed with an electric mixer or 100 strokes by hand with a wooden spoon.
5. Gently fold egg whites into cake batter. Blend thoroughly.
6. Pour batter into 2 greased 8-inch cake pans.
7. Bake on center rack of oven for 15 minutes or until knife inserted in the middle comes out clean.
8. Remove from oven when done. Cool for 10 minutes then remove cakes from pans. Cool on a wire rack until cakes are at room temperature.
9. Cover first cake layer with fruit. Add second cake layer.

10. Spread whipped cream on sides and top of cake.
11. Chill for 2 hours before serving. Garnish with maraschino cherries.

Swiss Roll

Ingredients
4 egg yolks
¾ cup sugar
1 teaspoon vanilla
¾ cup flour
¾ tablespoon baking powder
½ teaspoon salt
4 egg whites
½ cup strawberry jam
½ cup walnuts (optional)

Note: Instead of jam, you may fill with ice cream, whipped cream, or chocolate spread (such as Nutella).

Preparation
1. Preheat oven to 375°F.
2. In a large mixing bowl, beat egg yolks, sugar, and vanilla until smooth.
3. In a separate bowl, sift flour, baking powder, and salt.
4. Gradually add flour mixture to egg yolk mixture.
5. In another bowl, beat egg whites until stiff; fold into flour mixture.
6. Grease a 13x9x2 rectangular pan; add cake batter and bake for 13 minutes.
7. Meanwhile, cut a sheet of wax or parchment paper a bit larger than cake and sprinkle with powdered sugar.
8. Remove cake from oven and immediately loosen cake from the pan using a spatula and knife.
Note: Cake will be very sticky if allowed to sit in pan.
9. Turn pan upside down onto the wax paper, cutting off any excess paper. Using the wax paper around the cake, gently roll up the entire cake until it resembles a log. Chill in refrigerator for 1 hour.
Note: If you are using ice cream as a filling, place in the freezer for 5 hours before serving.
10. Unroll the cake and spread jam in an even layer on top of the cake. Roll the cake back up again this time omitting the wax paper. Chill in refrigerator for at least two hours.
11. Serve cold.
Serves 12

Burnt Milk Pudding with Chicken Breasts
Tabuk Goğsu Kazandibi
Ottoman Empire

Ingredients
½ lb chicken breast
4 tablespoons fine-grain corn flour
3 cups milk, room temperature
1 cup half and half
¼ teaspoon salt
¾ cup sugar

Preparation
1. Place chicken breast in a saucepan with 2 cups water; bring to a boil over medium-high heat, skimming off any foam that may form. Reduce heat to medium-low and simmer until the meat is cooked. Drain and shred into fine threads
2. In a bowl, combine corn flour and 1 cup of the milk.
3. Pour remaining 2 cups of milk into a saucepan. Add half and half, salt, and sugar. Bring to a boil over medium heat, stirring constantly. Remove from heat.
4. Slowly add corn flour-milk mixture in a trickle to the pot, stirring constantly.
5. Simmer over medium-low heat until the mixture begins to thicken, stirring constantly to avoid scorching. Cook until pudding is a very thick consistency about 20-25 minutes.
6. Remove from heat and add shredded chicken.
7. Preheat heavy-bottomed frying pan over medium-low heat.
8. To burn the pudding, pour it into a frying pan and leave without stirring for 10-15 minutes.
9. Remove from heat, leave to cool in the pan.
When cooled, cut the pudding into rectangles and roll into logs.
10. Serve at room temperature or slightly cooled.

Serves 6

Beverage Chapter

Zam Zam Water

One year Hajjah Naziha traveled to Mecca on Hajj with her mother Hajja Anne and her two sisters in law. When they arrived in Mecca they were so exhausted they had to sit and rest. Someone brought them some Zam Zam water as a refreshment. Hajjah described how she felt instantly revived and full of energy to fulfill her Hajj.

Arabic Coffee
Middle East

This coffee is served after large meals; especially in the afternoon after a large lunch. In order to prepare this you will need a set of Arabic coffee cups and preferably an Arabic coffee maker. Both the cups and the coffee maker are widely available at Mediterranean markets. If not, you can substitute espresso cups and use a small pot with a pour spout to brew it.

Ingredients
Arabic coffee
water
cardamom seeds (optional)
sugar
orange blossom water (optional)

Preparation

1. For each serving, measure 1 Arabic coffee cup of water into the coffee maker. For example, for 3 servings, fill 3 Arabic coffee cups full of water and pour into the Arabic coffee pot.

If desired, add 2-3 cardamom seeds to the water. They lend a nice flavor and aroma to the coffee.

2. To make the coffee sweet, add 1½ teaspoons of sugar for each cup of water. For mildly sweet coffee, add 1 teaspoon of sugar for each cup of water. For slightly sweet coffee, add ½ teaspoon of sugar for each cup of water. For a bitter coffee, add no sugar at all.

3. Stir the sugar into the water until it dissolves. Bring the water and sugar to a boil over medium-high heat.

4. When the water comes to a boil, remove the coffee maker from the heat. Slowly stir in 1 slightly heaping teaspoon of coffee per cup and return to the heat.

When the mixture comes to a boil, remove from the heat immediately. Foam will be produced rapidly once it starts to boil, be careful the mixture does not boil over.

Note: A long-handled teaspoon makes it easier to add the sugar and the coffee because your hand does not get as close to the heat from the coffeepot, but a regular-size teaspoon will work as well.

5. Stir the foam with a spoon to break up the bubbles thereby reducing any foam.

Arabic people generally do not like foam in their coffee.

6. Return to the heat and once again remove when the mixture comes to boil; stirring to reduce any foam that may form.

7. If desired, add a couple drops of orange blossom water to each Arabic coffee cup before pouring the coffee into the serving cups.

8. Pour the coffee into each cup, a little into each cup at a time, so no one gets the "bad" coffee (the grounds) at the bottom. The best part of the coffee is considered the top part, and the worst part is considered the bottom part.

9. Serve hot.

www.ingramcontent.com/pod-product-compliance
Lightning Source LLC
Chambersburg PA
CBHW041111070526
44584CB00002B/134